"*Parenting with Heart* is a rac
ents and grandparents, who k
easy. It is foolish to believe soi
can be legislated into a few step~ ~~ p~~~~~pic~. james and Dodd
offer a map to guide your engagement with your children and the
wisdom to do so humbly, even in the face of inevitable struggles.
Parenting changes us all, but often it turns us more toward guilt
or worry. This brilliant resource will give you a path for joy and
rich relationships with your children. You (and your children) will
not be the same after reading this book."

> **Dan B. Allender**, PhD, professor of counseling psychology
> and founding president of The Seattle School of Theology
> and Psychology; author of *Healing the Wounded Heart*
> and *How Children Raise Parents*

"Stephen James and Chip Dodd have invited you into their counseling offices in this book. They have created a safe space for you
to grow as a parent—to learn, to laugh, to be honest about your
vulnerability and imperfection, and to discover. You will finish this
book with more hope, more understanding, and more grace—for
both your child and yourself."

> **Sissy Goff**, MEd, LPC-MHSP, director of child and adolescent
> counseling, Daystar Counseling Ministries; speaker; and author
> of numerous books, including *Are My Kids on Track?*

"Every beleaguered parent who reads this book is going to let out
a massive sigh of relief. Finally, a book that is not telling them
what to do and how they are not measuring up. Stephen James
and Chip Dodd do a masterful job of defining God's high calling
in the life of a parent without adding to their collective sense of
regret and guilt for not being 'perfect.' I had to laugh out loud
when I read the subheading, 'Clumsy is as good as it gets!' And
all the parents said, 'Amen!'"

> **Jimmy Myers**, PhD, LPC-S, coauthor of *Fearless Parenting: How
> to Raise Faithful Kids in a Secular Culture*

"I trust Chip Dodd and Stephen James. I trust and value their
work as counselors and teachers. More importantly, I trust them
as people and as fathers themselves. These wise men are inviting
us into a more sustainable way to parent the kids we love, whatever
ages they may be. Chip and Stephen are showing us how to be
clumsy and courageous at the same time. I will recommend this

book to countless parents, and I'll be revisiting this rich content as a dad myself."

David Thomas, LMSW, director of family counseling, Daystar Counseling Ministries; coauthor of eight books, including *Intentional Parenting*

"Chip Dodd and Stephen James understand the intricacies of the heart better than just about anyone I know. Interweaving the relationship with one's self, one's child, and with God into the process of parenting is the foundation of this book. Through their writing, Chip and Stephen elevate relationship over the technicalities and product of parenting."

Amy Graham, MTS, pastor of spiritual care, The District Church, Washington, DC

"Stephen James and Chip Dodd's newest book, *Parenting with Heart*, is truly an outstanding endeavor! Besides being very informative, it provides an interesting and unique perspective on what it takes to be a successful parent and to raise healthy, happy children. It's one of the best parenting books I've read in a long time. Every parent needs this book in their tool bag!"

Rick Johnson, bestselling author of *That's My Son; Better Dads, Stronger Sons;* and *10 Things Great Dads Do*

"This book is a wake-up call to stop striving for perfectionism and instead become the parent who can win the heart of your child. This is a challenge to lead with vulnerability and to allow your weaknesses to be turned into strengths. You will not regret going on this journey with Stephen James and Chip Dodd, who are such respected leaders in their field. If you are like me, camping out in this book will impact not only your parenting but also your soul."

Aaron Graham, DMin, lead pastor, The District Church, Washington, DC

"As Stephen James and Chip Dodd so effectively articulate, parenting with heart is infinitely more wonderful—and more challenging!—than trying to control our kids' behavior and future. While we may think having happy, successful children is the highest goal, that's a poor substitute for raising kids who can love and learn from life on life's terms. Stephen and Chip share vulnerably from their own parenting journeys, guiding those of us who long to embrace the adventure and freedom of being full-hearted parents. In reading this book, you will grow and be transformed, which means your children will grow and be transformed too. Don't settle for endless striving to be a 'perfect' parent. Follow Stephen and Chip and be a gloriously clumsy, fabulously good-enough parent instead."

Dr. Jeramy and Jerusha Clark, authors of several books, including the award-winning *Your Teenager Is Not Crazy: Understanding Your Teen's Brain Can Make You a Better Parent*

"If you are looking for a parenting book that allows you to gain insight into your children's future, then read *Parenting with Heart*. The book guides you, the parent, to first look at your heart and identify your imperfections. When you shift inward, seriously considering your own flaws as a parent, you begin to move to a posture of passion and surrender to be more fully known by your children. Stephen James and Chip Dodd have put in the 'heart' work and energy needed to make this book a challenging read. Looking inward can be heart wrenching and difficult, but through their coaching and your own 'heart' work, you will find that it is definitely worth it."

Rhonda W. Smith, MEd, middle school head, Christ Presbyterian Academy

"If as a parent you wonder how much of your past and upbringing comes to bear when raising your own children, read *Parenting with Heart*. We all carry the baggage of our childhood experiences forward into how we parent our children. But taking the time to look back and examine our own 'junk'—as painful as that may be—allows us to take a fresh view of where we are now and where we want to go with our children. Take the time to read Stephen James and Chip Dodd's thought-provoking book, and use it as a guide as you make the journey inward that will propel you and your family forward. You won't regret it!"

Nate Morrow, MEd, headmaster, Christ Presbyterian Academy

"Every parent who wants to full-heartedly love their child needs to read this book. This wise resource will encourage, confront, guide, and challenge you to engage your child in ways that are both gratifying and transforming to you both."

R. A. Dickey, Cy Young award-winning MLB All-Star and father of four; bestselling author of *Wherever I Wind Up: My Quest for Truth, Authenticity, and the Perfect Knuckleball*

PARENTING
with HEART

PARENTING
with HEART

How Imperfect Parents
Can Raise Resilient,
Loving, and Wise-Hearted Kids

Stephen James
and Chip Dodd

a division of Baker Publishing Group
Grand Rapids, Michigan

Published by Revell
a division of Baker Publishing Group
PO Box 6287, Grand Rapids, MI 49516-6287
www.revellbooks.com

Printed in the United States of America

Library of Congress Cataloging-in-Publication Control Number: 2018014426

ISBN 978-0-8007-2939-4

The names and details of the people and situations described in this book have been changed or presented in composite form in order to ensure the privacy and confidentiality of those who have shared their stories with the authors.

18 19 20 21 22 23 24   7 6 5 4 3 2 1

To our children in hope

Contents

Acknowledgments

Writing a book is a lot of hard work. This book is no exception; it has been literally decades in the making.

Our deepest gratitude goes most of all to the women we get to parent alongside—Heather and Sonya. For sure, most of who we are as men and parents can be traced back to their love of us.

A close second is our gratitude for our children. To quote Frank Sinatra, "Mistakes, [we've] made a few." Their individual willingness to forgive and accept us as fathers is a sweet foretaste of God's endless mercy and has helped us learn what it means to love with our whole hearts.

We'd like to thank Heather Ebert, who helped us with the initial outline and proposal, as well as our literary agent, Greg Daniels, who found our manuscript a home at Revell.

Thank you to the team at Revell for their hard work. People such as Vicki Crumpton labor in the background to bring life to ideas and ideas to life.

Finally, we want to acknowledge our patients over the years at the Center for Professional Excellence and Sage Hill Counseling who have lived into the hope and possibility of living wholeheartedly. The world is a better place because they took the risk of living fully, loving deeply, and leading well.

Introduction

Rarely do parents not want what's best for their children. We go out of our way to do right by them. We provide. We pray. We worry. We hope. We dream. We lose sleep. We spend hours of our lives driving from school to practice to friends' houses. We invest deep emotional energy worrying about their futures. We make solemn oaths to do even better than our own parents did. And parenting never ends.

Once we become a parent, we have accepted the ultimate full-time job. There are no vacations. No paid time off for putting in extra hours. Life keeps happening. Being a parent is not something we can ever stop being. Our call every day is to continue to show up in our own lives and in the lives of our children.

This does not mean we don't need breaks from the responsibilities of our daily lives for replenishment, because we do. And because parenting is such a long-term proposition, we need to pace ourselves and take a long-term view. If we as parents have a mind-set focused on the long haul, we are more available to engage our children with wisdom.

We need to approach parenting like we are trying to raise really wise fifty-year-olds, which means that we accept that when our children are younger, they aren't yet good at living life with skill and wisdom. How could they be? They are inexperienced. They're children. Parenting with an eye on the future is a very different approach than trying to manage eight-year-olds.

So much of who our children will become at fifty is shaped by their life experiences more than by how we teach them to behave. If they are to grow into people of integrity, compassion, courage, and wisdom, then they need help in knowing how to keep heart. They need our help as parents to keep their hearts open to life and God. If we do that, they will very likely be capable of extraordinary love as fifty-year-olds.

When Michael and Samantha (not their real names) found themselves in my (Stephen's) office for marriage counseling, they'd been married for twelve years and had three children under nine. They were bright and earnest and obviously cared for each other and shared a deep love for their children, but they were anxious and unsure of each other as parents. Their genuine care and concern for their children was evident—as was the growing conflict in their marriage surrounding parenting issues. Samantha wanted to make sure her children were okay, while Michael wanted to be sure his wife was okay, but in reality, nobody felt okay.

Like many couples, they had entered counseling in hopes of learning to "communicate more effectively" and "get things figured out." What they soon came to realize was that communication and figuring things out weren't really the issue. To be honest, Michael and Samantha were missing more than they knew. They lacked:

- a viable vision for their family
- a clear understanding of their stories
- a durable worldview that could carry their family the entirety of their lives
- practice engaging each other's hearts in meaningful ways

They were holding tight to their dreams of what they wanted their family to be but were quickly realizing that their life together as parents wasn't what they had hoped it would be.

Samantha remarked, "I thought that if I got married, I wouldn't be so lonely. Our relationship used to be so happy, and I thought having kids would just add to that. But I never knew it would be this hard. I love Michael and the kids so much. I can't understand why it's so difficult."

Michael and Samantha had each grown up in what they called good families, but neither could truly appreciate how ill prepared they were for the emotional challenges of life. They were largely out of touch with their own hearts, and they didn't know how to show up for themselves or for each other in any real, living, tangible way.

Over the next several weeks, Michael and Samantha made a lot of progress. As they explored their stories, they began to see how they had spent years trying to control each other's feelings and needs—something they had learned well in their families growing up. They realized how this actually kept them from being themselves, and how it left Samantha riddled with anxiety and Michael resigned in self-doubt. Their commitment to having a *happy* family was ironically the thing keeping them from the deeper connection and emotional freedom they truly desired.

"How do I avoid doing this to our kids?" Samantha asked.

"How can we change this for them?" Michael wondered aloud.

As parents ourselves, we understand all too well this craving for happiness. It's an idea that is often expressed by our clients who have little humans in their care. We also understand the deep desire not to mess up our kids. These desires and cravings express our love for them. The bad news is that by trying so hard to avoid the cycles of the past and not face the struggles of the present, we are almost guaranteed to repeat them. As professional counselors, we encounter individuals and couples like Michael and Samantha all the time—people who love each other and their children deeply but who discover that their resistance to life's heartache and the attempts to control life's realities and inevitabilities tend to create more problems than they avoid.

When we parent from a posture of anxiety, control, avoidance, or shame rather than from a posture of passion, vision, presence, and surrender to God, we inadvertently create more confusion and pain. We end up unintentionally and unknowingly harming our children—the exact opposite of what we hope to do. Only through an outgrowth of our own emotional and spiritual presence do we have what our children really need.

Our natural tendency is to want to be successful parents. The problem with this is that we ultimately measure ourselves by comparison (social media) and accomplishments (degrees). We have to get off the ladder. Not until we begin living fully, from the inside out, can we be present to each other and our children.

We will never have everything we or our children want. We must come to a place of accepting that we do not have the power to give each other or our children everything we wish or dream, nor do we have the ability to be perfect. As we awaken to the reality of our imperfections and accept them (and even celebrate them), we learn instead to parent from the heart.

Parenting from the Heart

As children grow and develop, parenting becomes even more complex. We want our kids to flourish physically, intellectually, psychologically, emotionally, and spiritually. We hope to nurture passion, a capacity for intimacy, and the character of integrity so that they become capable grown-ups who contribute to the world around them.

Though our goals as parents may be similar, the means we use to attain those goals run the gamut. All the conversations about best parenting in our contemporary age center on this question: What is a more authentic, helpful, and sustainable way to parent our children? Over the past decades, we have seen a cultural shift from a parent-centric household, in which children were raised to be obedient without protest of any kind (i.e., seen and not heard), to a more child-centric household, in which children's self-esteem is valued as the key to a happy adulthood (i.e., everyone gets a trophy).

What we propose is another way to parent that is neither parent-centric nor child-centric but heart-centric. In this approach, all members of the family relate to one another by using the voices of their hearts. Everyone in the family has equal worth but not equal authority. There is a lot of tension inherent in this idea. This approach requires more grace, commitment, and patience, but we believe the effort is worth it. As we parent our children from the heart, we find the space and the freedom to accept ourselves as parents who may not be perfect but who are good enough. And "good enough" is what we propose is the most excellent way.

Clumsy Is as Good as It Gets

A metaphor we like to use to describe this approach to parenting is that of giraffes running on ice. Giraffes on ice are out of their element; they're equipped for the savannas, not the subarctic. Giraffes on ice, with their tangled legs, spun-out bodies, and frantic faces, reflect back to us how we feel on a daily basis as we raise our children—an apt metaphor for guaranteed imperfection.

All of us are works in progress, and being a clumsy parent is as good as we will ever become. Sometimes we crash on the ice in a massive tangle, and sometimes we glide along, believing we will never fall again. We are powerless over being human. We are powerless over being imperfect. We are powerless over being deficient. As beautiful, mysterious, and magnificent as we are created to be, we are also created with astounding limitations, one of which is our inability to have mastery over life.

This sense of imperfection and powerlessness is key to becoming capable of loving a child in all their own humanity. We display this act of courage when we step onto the ice and embrace the beauty of living, loving, and leading truthfully, no matter how difficult.

How do we get to a place of accepting our powerlessness and imperfection while still pursuing all that is good, true, noble, lovely, just, admirable, and praiseworthy? There is no magic pill, no miracle cure, no checklist, no performance plan to arrive at this place of acceptance—only a path to walk and a life to live. This process of learning to live fully helps us to be good at being a person, which allows us to be the parent our children need. This is what we hope to offer in these pages.

This is not your typical parenting book. We won't describe what kids need at different developmental stages of their young lives. And we will not burden you with more to-do lists and scripts to perform (though we do offer some very practical and useful questions for you to ask yourself and real-life examples for you to consider). There are many resources to help you learn how to nurture your children at each of the formative stages. And there are shelves of books at libraries and bookstores to help you practically implement those plans with your kids. But without heart, all the knowledge and tools in the world won't give your children what they are made to receive. Rather than duplicate those efforts, we have laid out a path that will lead you—your true self—and your children through every phase of life. This wisdom will complement those other parenting resources and will make their teachings and techniques more effective.

It's hard in our compassion- and performance-driven culture to believe in our inherent imperfection when our social media profiles portray a seemingly glowing family life. (Who wants to post the pre-dinner temper tantrum—the one thrown by the parent?) Real life is what's happening behind closed doors in between the rosy posts on social media.

We invite you to a way of living in which you realize you cannot attain perfection no matter how hard you try. If you are ready to embrace the fact that no matter how loving and well-intentioned you may be, you will fall short of anticipating and meeting all your children's needs, this book is for you. If you can humbly accept the reality that you will wound your children, whether you intend to or not, this book is for you.

Our passion is to lead people back to their hearts so they can live more fully. This same gift was once given to us, and it's the heart behind this book. This book is about your heart as a parent. If your children don't have your heart, they will have to raise themselves based on your rules instead of relationship. Loosening your grip on the lists and the formulas may be unnerving, but our suggested approach is so much more promising. No matter your background, personal experiences, age, or children's ages, you can apply this heart-centric process to your life. Even if your kids are grown, it's not too late to grow as a parent or to be more involved in your children's hearts. We assure you it's never, ever too late.

This book is our appeal to parents to consider their relationship with their children as a lifelong relationship of love—one in which the ultimate fruits cannot be fully noticed for decades. We hope to lift parents out of the postures of anxiety and shame through which they so often relate with their children and ask them to consider a guiding question as a lantern to light the difficult and uncertain path they are on: What does it mean to parent a child toward being a full-hearted fifty-year-old?

Another Parenting Book?

In counseling sessions and during seminars we have taught, we have been asked repeatedly to write a parenting book from the perspective of the Spiritual Root System (SRS). Developed by Chip, the SRS is an integrative way of understanding ourselves holistically. Building off a metaphor in Jeremiah 17:5–10, the SRS synthesizes common themes of Christian theology, counseling psychology, neuroscience, philosophy, and the arts in order to help make sense of life's relational complexity. Simply put, the five roots of the human heart are feelings, needs, desire, longings, and hope. By addressing our roots and from where they draw their nourishment, we begin to live free—not bound by the narratives of our pasts or our biological drives—and our lives become fruitful.

For years, we resisted this request. One of the questions we asked ourselves when we started thinking about writing this book was "Why does anybody need another parenting book when there are already hundreds out there—most of them really good ones?"

Something else we considered was whether parents would really read a parenting book that is about parents and not about children. Most parenting books are about children (as most people would expect) and not about the parents. After all, who wants a parenting book that is not about children and doesn't offer solutions?

Most often parents turn to writers who claim they know what they're doing. Authors often proffer a list of the right things to do. (And who wouldn't love to have a list to follow?) Do these things and when you complete the list, you have a product called an adult. But in regard to the heart of parenting and the heart of a child, there isn't a list we can follow—just principles to practice in daily living.

Understandably, we want some kind of game plan, checklist, or instruction manual to help us be what our children need, but there is no perfect parenting model that will guarantee success or warrant our children (or us) against heartache. If a parenting book guarantees an outcome for a child's heart, the author is lying. In the Old Testament book of Leviticus, the Israelites received a list for many facets of life: how to treat foreigners and neighbors, conduct business, harvest crops, and a few dozen other things. Nobody could adhere to the lists. Paul wrote in the New Testament letter of Romans a detailed list for how to love and be at peace. The people who received the letter couldn't adhere to the list. In fact, Paul said he gave them the list so that they would know they couldn't follow it and would wind up understanding their need for God's grace.

Raising full-hearted children is not an outcome as much as it is a by-product of being our God-given true selves as parents. We can't help but raise kids with heart if we are parents with heart. So many parenting approaches focus on the outcome (kids). Far too few focus on the experience of parenting. That is the fundamental problem in parenting. We can know a ton about what our kids need and how they develop and how to best respond to them, but if our hearts are not in the right place, all those actions are, as the apostle Paul said in a letter to encourage Christians in Corinth, "a resounding gong or a clanging symbol"—we are just making a lot of noise. Paul continued, if we have knowledge, insight, and faith but no love (i.e., heart), then we are nothing (1 Cor. 13:1–2).

Being a full-hearted person means being a person who lives life with enthusiasm, sincerity, humility, commitment, courage, willingness, acceptance, and a daily surrender to life on life's terms. Full-hearted people recognize that their ultimate purpose is relationship, and they work to develop intimacy with themselves, others, and God. They can attach deeply to others in relationship and are able to value and honor the inevitable losses in their lives. They are able to recognize when they have been relationally wounded and know where to seek healing. Full-hearted people are able to say, "I'm sorry," "I am wrong," "You are right," and "Will you forgive me?" They are capable of accepting their limitations and celebrating their gifts. They listen to their fear, trust it to help them prepare, learn from their mistakes, and ultimately risk in faith—even in their uncertainties. Full-hearted people live with passion.

Becoming a person like this and parenting from a posture like this demand great intentionality. Fundamentally, they require trusting that parenting is a process and a relationship, not a task that gets results—this is even how God parents us. Changing this paradigm is our biggest passion behind this book. We want as many people as possible to lean into this style of parenting and begin to parent with a full heart.

So when we committed to writing this book, we were sure that we would do so from a perspective that is both realistic and humane—realistic in that we address and acknowledge the tragedy of life and the faithfulness of God, humane in that we do not set false expectations for parents or make promises that cannot be realized or sustained. We wrote this book from a posture of compassion and honesty because little in this life is more complex and requires as much heart as parenting.

We have attempted to write a book that addresses parenting for parents, parents as people who are parenting rather than parents who are learning how to raise their children— because you can't raise a child unless you understand your own heart, your own story, and the feelings, needs, desire, longings, and hope that are the foundation of your emotional and spiritual life.

This book, then, is an invitation to understand your heart and how you are made (specifically within the context of parenting). We set forth the relational language and the tools that will carry you—your true self—and your children through every phase of life.

Inside Out Parenting

You will notice several themes woven throughout this book; ideas such as powerlessness, surrender, acceptance, story, suffering, hope, freedom, intimacy, and others will emerge time and time again. We have worked hard not to be redundant, but it's impossible to talk about one component of what it means to parent with heart without referencing something we have previously mentioned. The human heart is messy. There is no direct route to describe it.

We have provided, however, a structure that we hope is helpful. We have divided the book into two parts with five chapters in each section. The first half of the book focuses primarily on knowing your own heart, not just as a parent but also as a person. We talk about:

- how to forgo perfectionism in favor of being good enough

- ways you are designed to experience and use your feelings in relationship with yourself, others, and God
- facing and accepting all your own childhood experiences, the good and the not so good
- coming to terms with the inevitable pain and failures you are bound to face throughout your life, especially as a parent

In the second half of the book, we move from the inside outward—from the roots of the process to the fruits it produces. This movement isn't necessarily linear; our personal growth tends to move in oddly shaped concentric circles, moving closer to and sometimes farther away from our goals but always keeping in sight the common vision, which is to stay connected to our hearts and to those of our children. We encourage you to:

- care for yourself and your marriage so that you aren't trying to parent from a dry well
- listen to the sentence written on your children's hearts so that you can help them pursue their unique makeup
- nurture your children's ability to keep the voice of the heart alive and wise
- live in the mystery and tension of unanswerable questions so that your children are free to do the same
- keep a long-term perspective on how to raise well-loved children who become compassionate, fully engaged grown-ups

At the close of each chapter, we offer questions to consider and practical ways to practice this process in your everyday life.

Wise-Hearted Parents and Full-Hearted Kids

We are fellow parents stumbling, sliding, and sometimes gliding along the ice of parenting right alongside you. We have included plenty of stories of our own living to prove it.

We met in 1998 when Chip was developing the manuscript for *The Voice of the Heart*. We have since spent several decades guiding people through the process of reclaiming their hearts and living fully. Following that book's transformational impact on individuals, we have been planning for many years to bring this heart-centric approach to parents and families. Many people are now waking up to the crucial importance of being present with their families, developing healthy attachment patterns in their children, and living a life of vulnerability and authenticity without the toxic shame that makes us shut down our hearts.

Participants in our seminars and clients in our counseling offices who learn to engage their hearts ask the same question Michael and Samantha asked: "What about our kids?" Our answer is this: your kids need you—fully human and fully alive. You are the gift you give your children—the real you.

We continue to practice this process as parents ourselves, and we invite you to join us on the ice as we struggle and fall down and get back up and move forward. Our hope is to help you surrender to this process, gain acceptance of yourself as an imperfect human being and a good-enough parent, and relish being fully yourself and fully alive in relationship with your children.

Your dreams will always be greater than your abilities, but you will be blessed by facing your limits and by continuing to live in courageous hope. The gift of the effort is freedom—the freedom to persevere, to laugh at yourself, to be embarrassed, to experience regrets and forgiveness, to not take yourself so seriously, and to experience the profound and meaningful mystery of loving as you let go.

PART ONE

INSIDE
(Me with Me)

ONE

Giraffes on Ice

You're on Earth. There's no cure for that.

Samuel Beckett

A few years ago, I (Chip) was teaching a class at the Center for Professional Excellence, a treatment center for professional men who desire healing from addiction, depression, and anxiety struggles. Everyone in this group was highly intelligent, driven, and successful in their respective fields. They came from all walks of life. They were husbands, fathers, brothers, and sons. They were surgeons, pastors, dentists, and business leaders. These men had achieved much and given thousands of cumulative hours of service in their respective communities.

However, they also had something else in common: they were in the courageous and tentative first steps of recovery from addiction so they could have recovery of the rest of their lives. Like so many others, these men, before arriving at the treatment program, had attempted to pull themselves, their work, their families, their friends, and their multiple responsibilities up a sand mountain using nothing but their intelligence, willpower, moral purpose, and ego. The higher they got, the more exhausted they became and the more damage they inflicted on everyone around them as they slid down the drifting sand. They came looking for help in restoring their lives—if possible.

On this particular day, we were talking about the sand mountain of perfection—the mountain made of achievements we thought we should be able to attain if we tried hard enough, were blessed enough, or were helped enough. What a trap this sand mountain is! No one reaches its summit of perfection, and yet we are trained to judge or assess ourselves against its heights.

As I spoke, I began to imagine giraffes attempting to maneuver on a frozen lake—their gangly bodies sliding on the ice, legs entangled, necks bent, as they grasped for stability and control but all the while simply fumbled, bumbled, and finally crumbled to the ice. Then they got up again and again until they could finally do what was very unnatural to this creature unsuited for such an environment. I shared with them this image and the best news I had to offer: "You have to face the reality that clumsy is as good as you will ever become."

Nowhere is this idea truer than in the area of parenting. This may sound strange, but addiction recovery and parenting have a great deal in common. People in both groups need to leave the sand mountain of perfection behind and step onto the ice clumsily and yet courageously in order to live life on life's terms.

Just as a physician practices medicine, parents practice parenting. Just as an addict in recovery takes it one day at a time, parents have to lean into the mystery of not being in control of life. The best anyone ever becomes is good at practice. Being clumsy does not stop our desire for excellence, and yet it speaks to the conflict in which we live: life will never live up to what our hearts can picture. A willingness to embrace our limitations and experience our lack of control is essential if we want to live well ourselves and be in authentic relationship with a child—of any age.

Acknowledging we will be clumsy is the secret to parenting full-heartedly. We want our children's lives to turn out well and for them to be more successful than we have been. We want our kids to be happy, but they won't always be (no matter how great a parent we are). The reality is that children can never be more than their parents, nor can parents be more than their children. We all will always be human.

The great irony is this: the more we expect or demand to control the outcomes, the more out of control life becomes. We can push against this lack of control, but the realities of daily life push back against us. Believing we are in control of as much as we pretend to be is a kind of craziness—and it's considered normal because it's so common. True normal is powerlessness. True normal is not going to change; we must change by leaving the sand mountain and finding freedom on the frozen lake. However, we can become better people, better mates, and better parents by being more adept at being human.

This idea of being a giraffe on ice is not new. You don't have to go far to find it. Donald Winnicott is less recognizable in modern times, but he had a revolutionary effect on

PARENTING *with* HEART

parenting. Winnicott was a renowned psychoanalyst and child psychiatrist whom many consider to have been one of the most important early psychoanalysts. He was twice president of the British Psycho-Analytic Society and the first child psychoanalyst in Britain who was medically trained. He authored numerous enduring books whose material often originated in hundreds of talks he gave on BBC Radio and in person to social workers, clergy, teachers, and others who worked with children and families.

Through his teachings and writings, Winnicott introduced the concept of the "good-enough mother,"[1] a more nurturing approach to parenthood that left room for inevitable failures to be viewed not as an unfortunate reality but as part of what helps children grow into resilient adults. In Winnicott's view, the significant ills of society, from substance abuse to domestic violence to political extremism, were consequences of the failure to provide children with safe and supportive upbringings. The concept of being good enough wasn't meant to condone parental mediocrity; on the contrary, it was considered essential for society to thrive.

The "not-good-enough parent," by contrast, is one who needs the child to take care of him or her rather than the other way around. A child who is either ignored or forced to become the emotional caretaker will develop into an unhealthy person, one without a sense of being real and alive. The good-enough parent fosters a well-adjusted, creative, emotional sense of self in the child, who then feels more or less secure in the world. It's rare that any parent starts here. This idea of being good enough is something we come to only by recognizing and admitting our mistakes as parents.

I (Chip) didn't always know this. In my first steps into parenting, I wanted perfection, to prevent having to face the pain of mistakes and the pain those mistakes would cost my child. In 1988, my wife, Sonya, and I were about to have our first child. We were lying in bed, and I was thinking about the upcoming birth, which made me reflect on my own childhood. As I pictured what raising a son would be like, I became afraid.

"I want girls," I said.

"What are you talking about?" Sonya asked.

"Well, I don't want boys because boys will quickly know all I can't do."

She asked me again what I was talking about. I was imagining a game of catch in the backyard—a warm spring day, trees lining the fence, a picture-perfect day. All of a sudden my future son throws the baseball to me, but I don't get my glove in the right place and I drop it. And my son thinks something like, "My dad is so pathetic." My son is going to expect me to do everything well, know answers, fix problems, never be defeated, be heroic, and keep him from all harm in life. I will fail, and then what?

I told Sonya about how I would fail my son's expectations, and I would lose his respect and love. "You know," I said, "the American father and his son. *Field of Dreams.* That sort of thing."

Sonya was teaching third grade at that time, and she said, "Chip, I see dads come into my classroom who, frankly, some would think are unfit as human beings, not just as parents. Yet the kids look up and say, 'Dad!' and run to these men. You don't understand," she said. "There's no way your child cannot love you. Your child can't help but love you. So it's okay."

What she said made so much sense. I wanted to believe her, but I was resistant. (Of course, how mistaken to think that raising either a boy or a girl would somehow be easier based on gender.)

So I began to come to terms with the idea that my child would love me. But did that mean I had given up on the idea of impressing my son with my best-dad-ever act, with my perfection? Of course not!

Five years later, my son, Tennyson, was on the four-to-five-year-olds soccer team, which he and his friends really enjoyed. The dad of one of his teammates used to play college football. We would stand together on the sidelines and watch our kids play. At six foot four, I'm a pretty big guy, but next to him, I looked like a walking stick.

After practice one evening, Tennyson and I were walking in the woods behind our house. I saw a log on the ground, and from my vantage point, I could tell it was probably dry, rotting, and light but very big. I picked it up and looked at Tennyson as if to say, "Watch this, son." Then I heaved that heavy-looking log back into the woods. Thinking my feat was pretty impressive and feeling like one of those guys who compete in a telephone pole tossing contest, I gave Tennyson a "follow me—I'm your guy" nod of the head.

Unimpressed, my five-year-old looked at me and said matter-of-factly, "My friend's dad is stronger than that."

Wait a minute! I wanted to say. *Don't you know how many games his team lost?* But Tennyson had looked around the world and had seen that this other dad was physically stronger than me, in spite of my clumsy attempt to impress him.

I thought, *Parenting is going to be tougher than I thought and harder than I hoped.*

I didn't realize at the time that I was always trying to climb the sand mountain of perfection. I didn't yet realize that no matter how hard I tried to scale it, I would always come sliding back down. The best I had to offer to my son was that same mountain. No one achieves its summit of perfection, and yet I was trained to judge and assess myself against its heights. I didn't yet know the reality: clumsy was as good as I was ever going to get.

Two Bad Options and a Way Through

But who wants to be clumsy? Who wants to look like a giraffe running on ice?

In order to relinquish our agenda of creating a life for our children that is beyond reality, we must face the two stances of parental perfectionism with which we all struggle: achievement focused and comfort focused.

If we are an achievement-focused parent, we subtly (and not so subtly) baptize our children in the notion that if we/they learn enough, do enough, make enough, then we/they can make our/their lives work. Our motives, overtly or covertly, contain the word *perfect*. In this approach, there is rarely room for mystery, ambiguity, mistakes, struggle, disappointment, or even true wonder. Even worse, it's a formulaic approach to parenting that says, "If I give my children the right ingredients, and they do their part, then their lives will be ideally happy (as I the parent define it and wish for it to be)." Our actual agenda, whether acknowledged or not, is to prevent the pain of life happening to us.

Achievement-focused parents spend a great deal of energy trying to be great parents and have their children be great children. They are truly involved in training their children. They read books. They listen to podcasts. They go to seminars. They deeply love their kids, genuinely want what's best for them, and eagerly work and worry to make it so. Idealizing their children and their lives (or, might we say, idolizing them, because they really are the same thing) only sets up children for a powerful struggle with shame, inadequacy, and the compulsion to prove they are adequate or to give up. Because perfection is impossible, children will fail at completing the mission—the one their parents have set for them—and so they will fail their parents, fail their own mistaken expectations, and have a sense of failing others they love or need.

When we as parents need our children to achieve, we make our children idols. We shape and mold them into who we need them to be in a secret hope that they will make us okay. This achievement-focused perfectionism eventually diminishes a child's true self and shrouds the imago dei (i.e., how they are created as image bearers of God). No matter how good they look, what they accomplish, or how much they support our agenda, their hope that they will be accepted as they are created slowly ebbs away over time.

Often these achievement-focused parents become instructor/coach parents (hovering, watching, critiquing), challenging parents (demanding that the next obstacle of life becomes the next step of achievement for the child), or, even worse, a blend of the two: coaching-challenging parents.

The second model looks quite different on the surface but is very similar. This is comfort-focused perfectionism. Instead of being demanding of their children, comfort-focused parents demand perfection of the world around them. These parents attempt to create a place and a space in which their children will not have to experience life on life's terms.

These parents may allow *some* pain to enter their children's world, but most of all they encourage their children's absolute freedom of expression, with no discernment of how free expression differs from honest feeling and caring for others. Their children are given free rein to act on every impulse in the name of "keeping their identity." They are vociferously defended from any genuine outside feedback about their behavior—all in the name of love and self-esteem.

These parents give their children over to a world in which the children are god. The world needs to change for them, and they have few to no boundaries that would allow them to feel and process their feelings in healthy ways as real life occurs. These children grow up to be adults who lack empathy and resiliency. They also lack respect for others around them. Eventually, as a result of their refusal to experience life on life's terms, they bury their true selves in a deep pool of demands that life not be painful and difficult.

This deep pool becomes a grave for their true selves because they equate pain with failure and disappointment with terror. They believe happiness comes only when life works the way they think it should. These children become demanding adults who eventually sink because such entitlement cannot create a world into which they can integrate successfully unless they have complete control. Like the children of achievement, they become very demanding of relationships that don't fit their system of control.

While these may be extreme pictures, can you recognize the tendencies of either system in yourself—either as a child or as a parent? In reality, most of us as parents swerve back and forth between the polarities of these types of perfection-ism. Most of us ping-pong between these two dysfunctional models, and we become trapped between two equally un-tenable places—between a rock and a deep pool of water. These dispositions have nothing to do with socioeconomic, educational, or ethnic backgrounds. They have everything to do with the human heart and our willingness to face and feel life on life's terms.

This sounds heavy and ominous, doesn't it? It is. These styles of parenting can be overt, but more frequently they are subtle—one small seed of parental insecurity and per-fectionism planted at a time. If we dig down deep and give words to what is driving both types of parents, we might hear the heart say, "If I do this well, and I shape my children for success or safety or significance, then they will not hurt and will be happy and I can rest in knowing I did my best."

If we went even deeper, we might hear the heart say, "I don't really trust God to order the world of my children and care for them. I can do better than God. And even if I did trust God yesterday, today is a new day, and all kinds of mishaps and grief could befall them. Sunburn. Toothaches. Pimples. Heartbreak. Friend betrayal. Not to mention child-hood illness, painful injuries, sexual abuse, or death. No thanks. I'll write this story. I know better." All of which is understandable. It is just not how life works. Children are not created for parents to find success by protecting themselves in the name of caring for their children.

The good news is that there is a third way, a way through, a more heart-centric approach in which we let ourselves and our children be good enough—a concept that embraces a more integrated, authentic, and engaged style of parenting.

This way leads us away from the demands of perfectionism for ourselves, our children, or our world.

Rather than seeking to be safe and in control, we become capable of living life on life's terms. Instead of striving for perfection, we find rest in the reality that we will be, for the rest of our days, a constant work in progress, perennially unfinished, perpetually imperfect—always becoming in the experience of daily living. When we begin to accept that clumsy is the best we get—like giraffes on ice—we can begin to offer what our children really need from us: heartfelt relationship. This encompasses empathy, sensitivity, grief and celebration, perseverance, authenticity, understanding, boundaries, and reduced demands while still having high expectations, gratitude for others, gratitude for gifts they have, acceptance of others and self, understandable anger and frustration about life, and hope as what holds it all together.

This sounds like a lot—and it is. These noble things cannot be achieved through knowing more but only through gaining and surrendering to the heart experience of living. The good-enough, clumsy parent is a wise-hearted person—someone who lives from a place rooted deeply in their authentic emotional and spiritual core and who has struggled truthfully to accept this clear edict: it takes a lifetime to learn how to live. Living the way we are made to live means acknowledging our feelings and asking for help and confessing that we are human. Living fully requires the ability to struggle daily with this truth: if we are going to experience the joy of life, we cannot escape the pain of love. If we don't stay sensitive to life, then we revert to perfectionism—insisting that life and our children and other people behave according to our preset agendas.

Powerlessness: An Essential Ingredient

The very thing that most parents spend their lives trying to avoid is their powerlessness over what might happen to their children. Parents want to overcome this powerlessness so that they can protect their kids from experiencing the pain they themselves have encountered in their own lives or know could be encountered. To live courageously, parents need a vibrant and real spirituality and deep, abiding relationships with other adults who share this vision for living fully and parenting from the heart. If parents aren't talking to other grown-ups they trust about this struggle with powerlessness and anxiety, then their love will be weak—even cheap. Their children will become responsible for making them happy, and that turns children into something they're not.

If we stay sensitive to life, we will experience powerlessness, which becomes a doorway to true spiritual and emotional growth. Admission of powerlessness is the key that unlocks the door into relationship with God, our friends, our spouses, ourselves, and our kids with room for mistakes and forgiveness. Our children need to know that we have the emotional capacity to be present with them during the greatest struggles and trials and the greatest celebrations. If we can stay in the struggle alongside our children and offer the assurance of our enduring presence, then they don't have to be anything other than human.

The primary function of parenting in the human drama is to help transform children into grown-ups, not to raise self-reflections of success or failure. Parenting is an emotional and spiritual calling that confronts us with our own egos, idols, and systems we construct to foster a false sense of security and control.

When we do finally take the risk of letting go of the outcomes (due to awareness, despair, or accident), we can discover the freedom of genuine clumsiness and its rich gifts of living fully in relationship, loving deeply, and leading well. It's only in the unscripted, serendipitous, and spontaneous moments of life that we are genuinely ourselves and genuinely experience who God is. We sense that we are in the hands of love. We come to trust that God is doing for us what we will never be able to achieve for ourselves.

Before we can live well as clumsy parents, we have to courageously step into imperfection. Giving up perfection means grief. In the grief, we find acceptance of the struggle, and we hope again. Only then can we more honestly move toward giving our children authentic lives instead of the idealized versions of who we think they should be. This surrender doesn't mean we don't desire our own or our children's best. It means we give them our true selves and help them nurture theirs. When children intimately know the heart of their parent, they become free to become themselves.

The Ultimate Gift

My (Chip's) mother gave me a great gift regarding clumsiness, though I couldn't realize the far-reaching bigness of it at the time. I was in the third or fourth grade and said something very mean to her, such as "I hate you" or "I can't stand you." I remember knowing how wrong it was to say those things, and yet I also remember being so glad that she could take it. I think I was testing her love, her capacity to handle all of me.

Her ability to tolerate my words was amazing. I remember that my mother responded with something along these lines: "This is the first time I have ever been a parent. I don't know how to do it all well. I need your cooperation and help too." She was telling me we were in this together. In so many words, she was saying this was our first time through life. Everybody has to learn. And clumsy is as good as it gets.

Imperfect parenting is a gift to you and your children. Not only are your children well supported, nurtured, and loved, but they are also inevitably frustrated by your failures and must adjust to living in a flawed and fallen world. These children come to understand that life may be difficult and disappointing, but they are also more resilient in the face of setbacks and pain. They can continue to hope while living between inevitable grief and real celebration. They have seen their parents do it. They have seen their parents seek forgiveness for not doing it too, which is, paradoxically, a wonderful form of being good enough. Being good enough offers children the opportunity to become unique individuals who integrate fully into the realities of life.

Presence Replacing Perfection

This is what really matters as a parent: Are you present? Is your heart open to the pain and the joy? Are you vulnerable to the powerlessness of what life may bring? Can you admit to running from life? Or do you try to control life or ignore its depth? Like giraffes on ice, we are creatures living uncomfortable lives because we are created with a deep longing for peace, home, and security and a passionate desire for intimacy. Life is uncomfortable and sometimes devastating and sometimes so full and rich that we want to freeze the moment forever. We must practice living life on life's terms because parents and kids alike will be broken by life. The most authentic gift we can give our children is the offering of our presence to ensure that they are not alone in their pain.

There is no such place as "away" from our kids or the pain in our lives. There is no place where we can escape the agony and still be alive to love and feel joy. Love is most present in hard times. Though the cost is great, our only solace and recourse is to love deeply, and loving deeply demands full presence, no matter what.

GOING DEEPER

- In what ways are you striving for perfection as a parent?
- In what ways do you keep a distance from your child's struggle with life so as not to face your own? If you are a parent to more than one child, think specifically in terms of each child.
- What do you do when you feel like you have failed?
- What does it feel like to know that all you can be is good enough?

TWO

Wired for Relationship

Love is our true destiny. We do not find the meaning
of life by ourselves alone—we find it with another.

Thomas Merton

Each fall, right around Thanksgiving, my (Stephen's) family takes a long vacation to the beach. We have been doing this each year for more than a decade. One year when our youngest children, Henry and Teddy, a set of twins, were not more than two or three, I remember them discovering the ocean for the first time. It was a calm, warm day, and the waves were gently breaking on the beach. Henry and Teddy would run to the edge of ocean, and just as the cold water would hit their toes, they would run giggling back up the beach away from the water. They did this for a long time, scurrying in and out with the receding tide.

The sun was just beginning to set, and the shadows were growing long on the white sand. They gradually grew more courageous, going out one inch farther at a time until the water was up to their waists. Now, granted, they were still very small and had no experience with the ocean. Suddenly, a larger wave surprised them and broke right into their faces, filling their mouths and noses with saltwater. They both ran crying to Heather and me, who stood watching a few steps away. We scooped them up in towels and calmed and reassured them. It wasn't long before they were back at the shore's edge, starting the drama all over again.

What a beautiful illustration of the interplay of God, life, children, and parents. This scene is in no way unique to my family. I am certain that you can find children and parents all over the world playing out a similar story. I can even remember a similar moment from my own childhood with my own parents.

Across cultures, ethnicities, races, and religions and up and down the eras of history, we humans are more the same than different. From a DNA perspective, we are 99.9 percent identical, even emotionally and spiritually. As we go back in time, thousands and thousands of years, we encounter humans who were very similar to who we are today. Recorded history continues to tell the same story of living, loving, and leading. It speaks of feelings, desires, longings, needs, hopes, dreams, agony, celebration, heartache, and heartbreak.

When I (Chip) was a PhD student at the University of North Texas, I worked for the university as a tutor. One day a very mature sophomore from India came to get some help. He ended up teaching me something I still remember thirty years later. As we talked, he told me that he and his father were in a book club and that one of the books they had read together was *To Kill a Mockingbird*, a novel set in

1930s Alabama. As he talked about the book, he began to cry because he knew what it was like for a culture to diminish the need of certain humans to belong and matter because of a .1 percent difference. His birthright and class separated him, and he cried about the pain of the caste system where he was from. *To Kill a Mockingbird* reminded him of his own experience of living. He related to Tom Robinson and Atticus and Scout and Jem and to a story of a culture he had never lived in or seen. And we were talking about a novel set in Maycomb, Alabama, written before either of us had been born. But I was from Tennessee and had seen racism in action firsthand. He and I sat there, having barely met, and he was crying about a way of life that was emotionally and spiritually similar to mine. Underneath the cultural, ethnic, racial, and historical separations, we were remarkably similar.

Many years later, Sonya and I were at a retreat for Olympic chaplains, coaches, and athletes. We sat down at a table for breakfast with a competitor and her husband. I asked her about her experience as an Olympian, about the emotional experience of training, loss, and victory. She courageously talked about how she had been moments away from winning a gold medal, and then she had crashed. Tears rolled down her cheeks as she talked about coming to the retreat to struggle with taking on another four years of training to get to the next Olympics. We listened to her story, both of us deeply touched by her struggle, her grief, and even her gratitude.

We could relate to her losses, having experienced plenty of our own and having walked through them with our sons. We had just met, but because she told her story and revealed her heart, we understood one another. The heart carries in it the truths of our similarities if we connect to the feelings of our experiences. That chance meeting turned into a correspondence between Sonya and the athlete for some time. Sonya would no more claim to be similar to an Olympian than I would claim to be similar to an astronaut. The similarities of the heart being revealed is what makes us related.

Our kinship of heart is so consistent that the chaplain who invited us to the retreat told us about how he cares for athletes from all over the globe the same way. He said, "I don't go to the Olympic Games to be a chaplain for the athletes as much as I go to conduct funerals. I go there to bury dreams. It's one funeral after another. All of these people have worked for years to get to this opportunity, and only three go to the stand, and only one really wins. And there are thousands of athletes there wanting that one thing." He attends funeral after funeral because loss is the same all over the world. We all feel, need, desire, long for, and hope. We all hunger to celebrate. We all have to grieve. This American chaplain has something to offer a Japanese gymnast because loss, celebration, and everything in between are the same no matter where we go, if we will only admit it.

Not only is this true across cultures in our time, but it is also true throughout history. In the Old Testament, King Artaxerxes said to Nehemiah, "Why does your face look so sad when you are not ill? This can be nothing but sadness of heart" (Neh. 2:2). The king spoke to a foreign underling, a cupbearer and a poison tester, with an understanding. The king looked at the "lesser" and recognized his own face, his own heart, his own life. That happened thousands of years ago in a foreign land in a completely different culture, and it still makes sense today. The frescoes and the masks from ancient Greece say the things we still identify with today: struggle, thriving, mystery, questions, agony, ecstasy, celebration, and grief. Faces that present the truths of the heart help us feel known, not alone, and akin to one another, regardless of where we are from and regardless of the time period. People from 2018 AD and 2018 BC are the same.

Every human is created as an emotional and spiritual creature, and we are created to do one thing in this life and only one thing. We are here to live fully. And the only way we can live fully is in relationship—with ourselves, others, God, and God's creation. Living fully in relationship creates as much fullness of life as possible. It even allows us to step out and do things in the world that end up benefitting the world.

The Old Testament book of Jeremiah says:

> But blessed is the one who trusts in the Lord,
>   whose confidence is in him.
> They will be like a tree planted by the water
>   that sends out its roots by the stream.
> It does not fear when heat comes;
>   its leaves are always green.
> It has no worries in a year of drought
>   and never fails to bear fruit. (17:7–8)

This ancient text paints a picture of how the human heart is created and how it is created to function. It says that if we are rooted in relationship with God and others, then even when adversity and struggle come our way, we still can be full and secure, we still have something to give because we have received. We are created with the capacity to experience need, trust, and abundance—not scarcity. We can thrive in heart and remain generous of heart even when things are hard if we are living in relationship from the inside out.

In verses 9–10, Jeremiah continues in a somewhat peculiar way. The author interrupts "what the LORD says" to add some editorial emphasis and insight by asking a question: "The heart is deceitful above all things, and desperately sick; who can understand it?" (ESV). It's as if when presented with two pictures of the state of the human heart—one living fully and one isolated—Jeremiah can't help but comment, "The way you say it, God, is so clear, but even knowing that truth people still choose isolation and death. The human heart is sick and self-deceptive. Can anyone ever understand it?"

To which the Lord replies to Jeremiah, "I can. You can fool yourself but you can't fool me."

> I the LORD search the heart
> and test the mind,
> to give every man according to his ways,
> according to the fruit of his deeds.

In effect, God answers Jeremiah's question and says even more. "Not only do I get it, but I also very specifically lay on the heart of each individual person what they need based on how they live." What an intimate idea: God's work in our lives isn't cookie-cutter or formulaic but individually tailored to each person.

The book of Jeremiah gives us a helpful metaphor to work with in order to engage not only our own hearts but also the hearts of our children. It compares a human being and the human heart to a tree. The roots of the heart are made to drink deeply so that the heart can grow into fullness.

The roots make up what is called our Spiritual Root System. Chip developed this model as a way of understanding who we are made to be so that we can do what we are created to do. There are five roots of the heart:

1. Feelings (of which there are eight core emotions) (Chip writes about these extensively in *The Voice of the Heart: A Call to Full Living.*)[1]
2. Needs (Chip expands on these in *The Needs of the Heart.*)[2]
3. Desire
4. Longings
5. Hope

These five roots make up the emotional and spiritual characteristics of a human being.

When a child is born, the child cannot help but do exactly what they are made to do. A child cannot help but use their feelings, needs, desire, longings, and hope to reach beyond their skin to connect with that which is going to allow them to be themselves. We are made to live from the inside out. We are made to reach out for connection from the inside out. The only way we find fulfillment is through connection to relationship, through intimacy with others who are living from their hearts.

Made to Attach (Belong and Matter)

All babies come into life reaching for connection. They want to intimately connect. They are made to bond. And parents are made to bond with babies because we are similarly created. Attachment theory is a way that psychologists describe the dynamics of long-term and short-term human relationships. Psychoanalyst John Bowlby was the first to talk about this, and Mary Ainsworth expanded on Bowlby's work when she broadly described four types of attachment: secure, anxious-preoccupied, dismissive-avoidant, and fearful-avoidant.[3]

We become securely attached by getting our needs met. Our greatest needs are relational. The two primary needs of all human beings are to belong and to matter. These two needs are as powerful as the needs for food, water, shelter, and clothing. We cannot meet these needs alone—they require relationship with others and with God.

We are made to belong and to matter to our parents and to others. These needs are met when who we are as emotional and spiritual beings is affirmed and confirmed. This is so fundamental that we spend our whole lives looking for these things. Nothing else will substitute. We are predesigned for relational fulfillment. We can't run from it. We can't prostitute it. We can't buy it. We can't rid ourselves of it. Every person (adult or child) can have their needs for belonging and mattering met only through genuine relational connection.

Most simply put, the need to belong is the need to be accepted as we are, as we are created. The need to matter is the need to be valued for what we bring to the relationship. Affirmation says yes to how we are created. Confirmation continues that acceptance with reinforcement of that essential yes. "You are made right." When a child is born, the child cannot help but do exactly what they are made to do. If the child's needs to belong and to matter are affirmed and confirmed, the child will attach securely.

These two needs (affirmation and confirmation) are so important that even Jesus, when he was about to start his ministry, went to be baptized by John. He went under the water, came up, and the voice from heaven said, "This is my Son, whom I love; with him I am well pleased" (Matt. 3:17). *He's mine, and I really like him.*

Remember passing notes in third grade that said, "I like you. Do you like me?" And you hoped the person would circle yes. Sometimes they'd act like they didn't get the note, which was like a nice no. We never outgrow this. A child's note captures something we experience throughout our lives. If we have enough yes in us, we can tolerate a lot of no from the world.

These needs to belong and to matter show up in marriage too. Based on this fundamental human need for acceptance, John Gottman, PhD, one of the most respected scholars and researchers on marriage, can predict a divorce with 90 percent accuracy largely by evaluating the correlation of positive to negative interactions in the relationship.[4] If members in a couple nod at each other, if they touch each other, if they use humor, if they laugh, if they are influenced by the other, they stay together. Couples can be cussing or blessing each other, but if there is a five to one ratio of positive to negative interactions, that couple will be stable. If the ratio is more than five to one, that couple is likely to be very happy. On the other side of the equation, even if the ratio is one-to-one positive to negative, there is a high likelihood that the couple is going to be divorced in the next few years.[5]

Marriages succeed and fail based on how well couples affirm and confirm each other. The opposite is also true. If a relationship is full of contempt, criticism, defensiveness, and stonewalling (what Gottman calls the Four Horsemen), the couple will likely divorce 5.6 years after marrying.[6] Now imagine how destructive these forces—contempt, criticism, defensiveness, and stonewalling (withdrawal)—can be in parenting.

Whether we are considering parenting or marriage, we are made to be affirmed and confirmed. We are made to be encouraged. We need somebody to say, "Yes, you are made just right." And then we need to hear it again. "Yes! Yes! Yes, you are made just right." In other words, we don't need to hear it once. We need to hear it the rest of our lives.

You Have to Have It to Give It

This idea that kids need to be loved and affirmed and praised goes well beyond activities and accomplishments. Children need to be accepted for who they really are—the essence of their character and personality. As parents, we can't give what we don't truly have. Therefore, if we don't really love ourselves and aren't truly known by others, then we can't fully love our children.

I (Stephen) remember when my daughter was about fourteen months old and we had moved from Nashville to Seattle for me to go to graduate school. This was a bold move for our young family. I was born in Nashville, Tennessee, and went to college in Nashville, where I met Heather, who grew up just down the road in Columbia, Tennessee.

After we moved to Seattle, I was going to school and working from home. It was fantastic. I was home a lot with Heather and our fourteen-month-old daughter, Emma Claire, and we'd spend the afternoons in the park. Now as a young adult, she tells a great story of a goose chasing me through the park because I had bread. The goose was honking and I was screaming. "You were screaming like a girl, Daddy," she recalls. I was running, throwing bread, trying to get away from the goose. It was a great season in our lives.

I remember giving her a bath one evening. She would play in the bath for the longest time. When it came time for me to take her out, she looked at me really deep in the eyes. I remember feeling this sense of shame. I didn't know what was happening, but I remember very quickly turning my head from her. It took months for us to reestablish the deep connection that she was looking for. She was safe. She was warm. We were playing. We were both just being ourselves. I'm a playful dad. But when she looked at me, I didn't want her to see how inadequate and insecure I felt as a man and as a father. I felt as if she was seeing into me. I felt exposed. I was early in my work of recovering my heart, and I had many wounds that I had not shared or found healing for. Because I couldn't stand myself, I couldn't let her stand me. I had to look away. I needed to turn away because she looked at me with admiration and delight and care and love. And she was drinking in my care and admiration and love. There was a sharing of cups being filled.

Children and parents are both human and both made of the same substance and with the same nature. We are all looking for the same thing: love, acceptance, affirmation, belonging. As parents, we need someone to look at us and say, "Yes, I see you. Yes, I like you. Yes, you are made of the right stuff." That is what children do, and that is what parents need. We are all wired for the same thing: to live fully in relationship. Those who are known the most get the most, but we have to be able to look into the face of being known.

As a young married couple, Sonya and I (Chip) attended a church in Flower Mound, Texas. At the end of each service, the minister would give a beautiful benediction: "May the Lord keep you. May the Lord bless you. May the Lord's face shine upon you and be gracious unto you." Then he would say, "Turn to the person beside you and give them the benediction." Sonya and I would turn, and we would look at each other face-to-face. She would look straight into my face and straight into my eyes and straight into my person with all her hopes and dreams, and she would say that beautiful blessing to me. I could barely stand it. I felt ashamed. I could hardly bear to look into the face of love. At that time in my life, I found it very difficult to receive such love, as I did not yet have the ability to give such love.

Good things happen to people who are known, people who can open their hearts to receive and give love. Whether in an experience of grief or celebration, we are connected by being known from the core of who we are, the heart of us. Good things happen to people who can articulate their hearts and tell the truth about themselves. They can offer themselves to the process of living life on life's terms, which begins with the need to be in relationship.

Those people make parents who can look into the faces of their children and allow their children to look into their faces. The ability to tolerate the powerlessness that love exposes in us is a good marker of our willingness and ability to tolerate the pain of love. Anyone we love will go through pain, and if we cannot deal with pain, then we cannot love well. The capacity to receive love is a marker of being a good, clumsy parent.

If we don't have that internal belief inside ourselves that we are made of the right stuff, then we are not going to be able to engage our children and the important people in our lives wholeheartedly and authentically. If we can't acknowledge that we are created a certain way, then we will attempt to get our needs to belong and to matter met through performance rather than through the presence of who we really are. Without a sense of deep intrinsic worth, all we can hope to do is perform well and fake it and teach our children to perform well and fake it. If we live bound in anxiety and/or oppressed by toxic shame, we will teach our children to reject who they truly are. Because children so deeply need to belong and to matter, they will try to change themselves into who they think they "should" be instead of becoming who they are created to be.

Wounds, Vows, and Losing Heart

When we teach the Spiritual Root System, we often get questions such as:

- If this is all so natural and prewired, what happened?
- How do I stop the cycle with my own children?
- What do I need to do in order to do a better job being myself with those who love me and need me the most?
- Why am I so defensive?
- What makes me so critical?
- What drives my contempt for myself and others?
- What triggers me to withdraw from relationship?
- How did I lose heart?

All of us have experienced emotional and spiritual wounds. This happens to everyone. Everyone gets wounded. There is nothing we can do to stop this from happening. Often when we are wounded, we get hurt and feel shame. Sometimes no one we trust is there to help us walk through the pain and shame and find healing and reconnection. In this loneliness, we respond by making vows. Though often quite simple, and often made in silence and in secret, these vows go a long way in helping us shut down parts of our hearts. We say things to ourselves such as:

"I won't let that happen again."

"They can't get to me."

"I'll never care that much again."

"I'm going to make sure I'm safe."

"I'm worth only what I can do for others."

"I'm loved only if I succeed."

"I'm better off alone."

To keep these vows, we construct emotional survival strategies to get our needs met without exposing our hearts. We get very creative in our survival strategies, often using the gifts of our intellect, willpower, and morality (being good) to become expert at hiding our hearts. We practice forms of being safe and in control instead of being truthful and present. We use our thinking to find ways to appease, please, caretake, seek approval, and achieve with others so we can be valued. Our effort and performance take the place of the presence of our true selves.

Performing for people for love takes the place of us being ourselves. This is emotionally and spiritually exhausting. We become isolated as a way of staying safe. We become survivors. The more emotionally isolated we become, the more self-centered we become. In our effort to protect our hearts, we hide them from ourselves and others. The price we pay becomes the cost our children will likewise pay. What your children need is the true, clumsy, beautiful, imperfect, authentic, struggling, forgiveness-seeking, noble you.

Let's take another look at the Spiritual Root System and Jeremiah 17.

This is what the LORD says:

> "Cursed is the one who trusts in man,
> who draws strength from mere flesh
> and whose heart turns away from the LORD.
> That person will be like a bush in the wastelands;
> they will not see prosperity when it comes.
> They will dwell in the parched places of the desert,
> in a salt land where no one lives." (vv. 5–6)

Here Jeremiah paints a stark contrast with the blessed person of Jeremiah 17:7–8. He shows us the cost of isolation and self-reliance.

One unique thing about humans is our ability to deny how we are made. No other creature can do this. Everything animate in life is unavoidably, unabashedly reaching to experience its fullness, its completion—its own living fully. This reality is true of trees, horses, and humans. However, humans have the ability through our amazing consciousness and intellect to hide the reality of how we are created. We have the power, creativity, and ingenuity to attempt to avoid the vulnerable expression of life's desire within us. We isolate ourselves. Unfortunately, we often use God's gifts of intellect, imagination, and willpower to hide what's in our hearts in order to avoid the pain of being imperfect, needy creatures who need relationship to thrive.

Sadly, many of us weren't raised in homes or in cultures where we were helped to express our hearts. We fear and distrust ourselves with others. We subtly (or not so subtly) deny or block efforts of relationship—and ultimately love—instead of being open. Closing off and isolating are understandable; however, our very real reasons and justifications do not change how we are created.

Unfortunately, we are in small and large ways often emotionally, physically, and/or spiritually abandoned by those we love the most. Sometimes we are trained (or train ourselves) to reject, deaden, or hide our hearts. And sometimes the only choice we have is to hide our hearts from ourselves and others in order to protect our true selves. Consequently, we don't know how to use our feelings, needs, desire, longings, and hope in order to live fully. We don't know how to handle those things that have wounded us. We become defensive, survival oriented, withdrawn, numb, and/or self-sufficient. And these tendencies interfere with our parenting ability.

Instead of expressing our hearts, we hide our hearts and attempt to bury our roots. In other words, we run from clumsiness. We run from being known. We run from having to be vulnerable to experience love and life and to give ourselves to somebody else—because when we do, we can get hurt.

When the roots of our hearts aren't fed the emotional and spiritual food of relational intimacy with ourselves, others, and God, our hearts do not thrive. They only survive. As damaging as this strategy of protection is to ourselves and to those who need us the most, it becomes the "best choice" we have until we become willing to change.

Double Whammy

All of us have attachment wounds. Few of us are what John Bowlby would call 100 percent securely attached. When we experience distress or get our feelings hurt (yes, that still happens to adults), we often move into some other less secure posture of attachment. We become anxious, dismissive, or fearful. We all have ways that we didn't and don't attach securely in relationship. This happens for two reasons.

One reason is because the people who were raising us (and/or the culture that was raising us) had their own impaired attachment styles. We didn't get the affirmation or the confirmation we needed because Mom or Dad didn't give it to us because they had shut down part of their hearts. Children develop maladaptive attachment structures based on how emotionally, spiritually, and/or psychologically impaired their parents are.

The other reason we may have an insecure attachment style is because we experienced some kind of emotional and/or physical trauma growing up. A very basic definition of trauma is the inability to make meaning of a negative emotionally impactful event. When we experience trauma, we become emotionally and psychologically dysregulated to the extent that we can't make sense of what happened. Trauma doesn't have to be what someone did to us, but it often is.

Trauma isn't just the obvious things like sexual abuse; physical abuse; sudden death of a parent, sibling, or family member; divorce; or a tragic childhood illness or injury. These "big T" traumas are significant, but there are also subtler "little t" traumas. These are often the common ways we mistreat our kids when we are stressed, overwhelmed, and out of touch with our hearts. Even normal parenting can shatter connection and trust with our children. Some examples are when a parent:

- plays mind games with a child
- rages at a child
- withdraws from/abandons a child (such as when a parent is in a severe depression, addiction, or illness)
- is consistently passive-aggressive and/or sarcastic
- has erratic mood swings and is emotionally unpredictable
- is one way at home and another way in public

When our wounds come from our parents or caregivers, they are really damaging. The little things can do a lot of damage. And when children experience this, they can't figure out why their hearts are saying yes but their hearts are also saying no at the same time. This creates a swirl of ambivalence in a child.

When the first (emotionally impaired parents) combines with the second (trauma), there is a real problem for a child. When the people we need to go to for help and to make sense of life's tragedies are not able to be present with us in our pain, fear, and shame, we are left emotionally and spiritually alone. Emotional abandonment and trauma interfere with (and sometimes, if the combination is bad enough, even shatter) our connection to ourselves, our connection to others, and our connection to God. When this happens, we have a disruption in our attachment to ourselves and our caregivers and in our trust in God.

No family escapes this heartbreak completely. Even the most common wounds can create significant damage. For example, a child in need comes to a parent and doesn't get a need met. (Often we won't even know this is happening.)

They try to start a conversation. "I want to show you what I've been doing . . ." And the parent is too busy doing something or too distracted by their own life stressors. Inside, the child may say, "Dad's too busy for me" or "Mom's too stressed out to be with me." The child concludes that they must be the problem.

Kids don't have the life experience to realize that the problem is with the parent. "What's wrong with me that Dad or Mom can't meet my needs? I must be too much. I'm too needy." The child feels worthless. This happens to every child who lives on the earth because every child has a human parent. Emotionally impaired parents or traumatic life events aren't necessary for this to happen. Every child develops toxic shame. Impaired parents and traumatic events just add to the depth of it.

Relational Duct Tape

Much of emotional woundedness can be mended, corrected, and healed through what's called a process reattunement, which is akin to emotional duct tape. This happens when a parent recognizes a relational breakdown and purposefully works to reconnect and be present with the child who is feeling disconnected, anxious, or insecure.

This process has some key elements.

1. Is the parent their own person? The process starts with the parent's ability to see themselves as separate from the child. If the parent can't be emotionally whole apart from the child's emotional disruption, then the parent can't help the child. If the parent can't withstand the

child's bad attitude or weather their sad mood, then there is little room for the parent to actually help the child remain attached to themselves, others, and God in a meaningful way.

2. Is the parent willing to seek and remain open to feedback? This feedback comes in two forms. First, it comes from the child. Children in emotionally healthy homes have a remarkable ability to protest. The parent needs to be able to tolerate, if even for a short time, the child's complaints, disappointments, and even at times disgust/hatred of the parent. Second, the parent needs to be open to seeking and receiving input from their spouse and from friends who are close enough and sage enough to tell them the truth.

3. Can the parent say, "I'm sorry"? The parent's ability to take responsibility for their actions and make amends is fundamental to remaining connected with the child. Can the parent take the risk of being wrong and seeking forgiveness—even from their own child?

4. Will the parent engage the child's heart? This last stage moves toward an active re-formation of connection and a rekindling of trust with the child as the parent addresses the inner world of the child as well as any boundaries or discipline of which the child is in need.

Notice that the first three elements take place in the heart of the parent. The more skilled the parent is in these first three elements, the more sincerely the parent can work to help the child repair relationship with themselves, others, and God.

One of my (Chip's) sons and I went on a fly-fishing trip a few years ago. He was out of college, gone from our home, and moving out into the bigger world. Near the lodge where we were staying was a great place to sit and watch the stars come out in the big sky of the West. We sat talking and watching the moon rise and the stars come out. I have always loved him, and he cannot stop loving me, as is the nature of children with their parents. That is what makes the wounds so deep and love's possibilities so rich. We talked about the day, the horses we rode, and the fish we didn't catch.

After a while, he said, "Dad, I used to be scared of you, but I'm not anymore." That courageous comment led to deeper and yet sadder talk about how I was harder than I should have been and more demanding than I ever needed to be. When he was growing up, I communicated expectations that made him feel he had to perform to receive acceptance. I remember my heart sinking and sadness filling me up. While he was referring to me no longer being like that, I recalled exactly what he meant. The last thing I would ever wish was for my own son, one of the greatest loves of my life, to feel he had to seek my approval and fear that it would not be his. But that is what happened.

I told him how sorry I was. He told me more, and I had to see more. We talked until the moon was far above us. What courage he had, and what trust he had in the possibilities of restoration and in my ability to respond with humility. I offered no excuses, no justifications. He knew my sorrow wouldn't become something he would have to carry, and he trusted me to show up in clumsiness and admit my failure. He knew that we are works in progress, and he trusted me to live this out, or he wouldn't have risked such vulnerability.

While I regretted harming his heart, I also trusted that forgiveness and mercy had more power in love than any performance I could ever script to make things okay.

Now we continue to talk as men who love each other, one a son, one a father, but more so two people who are clumsily approaching life as works in progress. He knew more than I did, and he was willing to share his heart. Good things happen to people who are known. I now have more of my son, and he has more of me. I can look into the face of love come what may. He showed me that truth.

How we handle conflict and what we do to repair relationship are essential to relational intimacy. Being able to tolerate another person's pain, anger, or fear—and being able to tolerate our own—actually makes the relationship closer and stronger than if there was never harm in the first place. This is the good news. The fact that children and parents are resilient in relationship is one of the greatest gifts of mercy God has given us.

Buckle Your Seat Belt—This Will Be a Bumpy Ride

My oldest son and I (Stephen) are working toward our private pilot's licenses. Our instructors emphasize the importance of the preflight checklist. Before each flight, we run through the same checklist to ensure that the plane is flight worthy. (There are even checklists within the checklist.) This process is a significant step, and a plane can be grounded for myriad reasons. One of our instructors will say regularly, "When you're flying, you have two bags: one bag of luck and one bag of experience. Your job as a pilot is to fill up the bag of experience before your bag of luck runs out."

That means getting knowledge, getting good instructions, and spending lots and lots of time flying. You can't learn to operate a plane without . . . well . . . operating a plane. I remember when we first started flying that I couldn't maintain a consistent altitude or heading. I would drift back and forth, up and down trying to stay my course. I flew more like a bee than a bird.

Parenting and piloting have a lot in common. We can't learn to parent without engaging the process and making a lot of mistakes.

Unlike piloting, parenting does not have a predictable checklist. There are not things to do and not to do that when completed produce a grown-up. (Wouldn't that make us all feel better?) When it comes to intimate relationship, there is no checklist. And if there were, we couldn't complete it. Being a parent is more of a path of life we are made to follow, not a list that is going to give us an answer.

Life's Big Question

The core human question comes back to a note many of us passed in the third grade, and in truth, we have been asking it our entire lives: "Do you like me?"

"Yes," someone responds.

Am I made the right way? we wonder. *Yes!* we hear back.

Do you like me? That is the question we are all asking, even as parents. When we have to discipline our children, a very human part of us is asking, "Hey, do you like me? Are we going to be okay after I discipline you?"

We all know the significant problem with parents who parent out of "I want you to like me." The other side of the coin, those who parent from "I don't care if you like me," is just as much of a problem. Our children are looking for affirmation and confirmation. And we have to be honest with ourselves: we are looking for the same things. If we don't have people in our lives we can talk to about what it's like to be a parent, then we are going to be in a really dangerous spot with our kids. Parents and kids are looking at each other with the same question: "Do you like me?" We need to hear a yes. One of the greatest things about being a parent is that our children will love us for who we are if we let them.

One of the greatest things we as parents and as people can do is to look into the face of love. How good are we at being known? Can we tolerate somebody looking into our hearts with love? Doing so can be very difficult.

GOING DEEPER

- Go on a walk as a family. Leave all electronic devices behind (but take the dog!). Enjoy the day winding down and your family being together. Ask each other questions, encourage every voice to be heard and valued, share both the highs and the lows of your day, and inquire about their day. Let your kids and your spouse know how much you care for them just by being with them and by being curious about them.

- Take a minute to look at yourself in the mirror. Look into your eyes. Then write a letter to yourself about all you see there, both the strengths and the struggles.

Include words to yourself as a child and what you wish your parents would have seen/spoken when you were young.

- Ask yourself, "In what ways do I allow my child to have their own identity with me?"

THREE

Living with
Unfinished Business

Can anything be sadder than work left
unfinished? Yes, work never begun.

Christina Rossetti

Middle school. Just the words on the page can arouse feelings
of insecurity in even the most confident person. Junior high
is a tough time. Masses of adolescents with hormones cours-
ing through their brains at unprecedented levels. Awkward.
Shameful. Bizarre. Confusing.

When I (Chip) entered junior high, I came from a small,
close-knit elementary school where everybody was the same,
and then we went to the middle school, where nobody was
the same. It seemed to me that everyone was thrown together
from everywhere and that nobody was really running the
school. School life seemed like survival of the fittest.

One thing I knew about middle school was that we could play football. I liked football, so I thought I would go out for the team. I didn't know football practice had started three weeks earlier. I thought it started after school began, like junior pro, which I had played the previous two years. So I found the coach and asked if I could go out for the team. He told me to come to the next practice.

The next day when I got there, it didn't take me long to decide that I was the wrong guy for this and that I wanted to quit. I could hardly breathe and couldn't catch up to what was going on, so I went to the coach and said, "I can't do this."

He said, "Yes, you can."

I said, "No, I can't." He told me to stand on the sidelines until practice was over. I was relieved knowing I would eventually get out of there. But then it dawned on me that I had to see my father later that night.

When my father got home, I remember looking in his face for a clue as to what mood he might be in. When I dared to tell him I had quit, his face seemed to sink. I knew I had come up way short of where I thought he needed me to be. If that wasn't bad enough, about that same moment it dawned on me that I was going to have to go back to school and face my classmates. Other boys knew I had quit. They knew I couldn't take it. Being perceived as weak and cowardly is not high on the list of middle-school boys, especially the older ones.

I didn't know the team had been practicing for three weeks. I was unprepared to move into the next stage of life. Already at fourteen, I was committed to not asking questions and trying to figure things out on my own. My approach of

"Just show up and do your best" had worked up until that point, but it didn't work anymore.

Apparently, my decision to quit was devastating to my father, because a few days later the coach called me into his office and said, "Your father is terribly disappointed in you. He wonders if you're made of the right stuff." I don't know if those were my father's words because I never asked and he never told me. Based on the look I had seen on my father's face, though, those words sounded true to me. Internally, they were like a sledgehammer to my heart. Then the coach said sternly, "I'm going to give you another chance."

I could hardly believe what came out of my mouth, but I said, "No." I knew I couldn't do it. I knew I didn't want to go back. Somehow I was angry and hurt enough to say no. I was also afraid because somewhere inside I knew I wasn't ready. From then onward, I believed I was certifiably inadequate and probably worse. Not only did I not make the cut, but I didn't even show up for it. I lived afraid from then on. I did make the basketball team the next year; I had always liked basketball. My father had always played football. He had even gotten an offer to play at Louisiana State University in the late 1940s. I knew that basketball wouldn't prove anything—no matter how good I got, no matter how much I sweated, no matter how hard I tried.

When I entered high school two years later and football tryouts came around, I knew it was time to take another shot. I wanted so badly for my father's face to change toward me. I couldn't articulate my feelings as much as I felt the face of acceptance or rejection, approval or disgust. "Okay, I've got to do it this time," I said to myself. "I've got to go out." As it turned out, the coach had a policy that there were no cuts in ninth-grade football. Anyone could go out for the football team and make the team if they could endure the first few weeks.

Eighty-eight went out for the team. At the end of three weeks, fourteen of us were left. Nobody was cut. The coach would run us and do drills until people quit. No uniforms were given out for two weeks. I remember running behind two kids named Jack and Eddie. "Are you quitting?" Jack asked Eddie.

"Are you quitting?" Eddie replied to Jack.

"Are you quitting?" they breathlessly asked each other.

I remember running behind them thinking, *I'm quitting. Y'all aren't asking me, but I've already decided. I'm through.* As we neared the field house, Jack and Eddie peeled off toward the locker room, and I thought, *Maybe I can get around the field one more time.* And I did. I wanted to go home so badly, but I knew in my heart something really scary awaited me.

During the rest of the season, I got hard, and I learned how to fake a toughness that made me acceptable. I also learned how much I didn't like football and that I didn't want to play. On the outside, I was tough. On the inside, I was still afraid. I could never prove myself enough to make me feel okay. I did not even like playing the game except in the backyard with my brothers and other boys from the neighborhood.

Fast-forward twenty-five years. My oldest son wanted to play baseball. He was really good. I remember one particular game. Tennyson was eight years old, and I was the assistant coach. Tennyson was pitching, and the opposing players started yelling mean things at him, stuff about how terrible he was. Then the parents started yelling at him, and then the grandparents started yelling at him.

I went out to the mound. I took with me my unfinished business to prove things from all my athletic days (which I didn't really grasp) and my personal vow that Tennyson was not going to have my story. My personal credo was "Don't let them get to you," and I had honed that since the ninth grade.

When I got to the mound, he was fighting tears the way boys do in front of their friends. I bent over and put my hands on my knees so I was almost eye to eye with Tennyson. "Do you want to do this?" (I was giving an eight-year-old boy a grown-up decision.) "Do you want to be here pitching?"

He answered, "Yes." Of course he did. I knew he would. He loved the game! He wanted to play, but he didn't know how to say, "Yeah, I want to play baseball, but I want them to stop." So he just said, "Yes." He gave me the *right* answer. The best I had to give him was my way of handling my unfinished business.

I said to him, "Listen. You just act like you can't hear a thing over there. You don't let them see that it bothers you. Okay? All right." I stood up and walked back to the dugout. I thought I was giving him some good stuff when in fact I was giving him my best defense mechanism, the way I had handled things since the ninth grade. I implanted in him this vow: "Never let anybody see you hurt. No matter what happens, you endure it stoically. Nobody touches your heart. As a result, you will be able to tolerate abuse from all the people around you as you go for your goal. You are going to achieve your goal and not let life get to you while you're doing it. You will not have to feel the pain I knew, because I love you."

Thankfully, the next day I awakened to the truth that I had done something harmful to my son. I had made him make a decision that an eight-year-old can't make. I had left him out on a mound to be by himself and endure alone. I hadn't had the courage to let myself feel beyond my survival mechanism to say, "Stop it now, ump," and to take the boys off the field. Not until the next day did I realize I could have handled things a lot differently. I had reacted out of my own unfinished business instead of responding to what my son needed.

To do things differently, I needed to pay attention to my unfinished business. I needed to think, *My old wounds are getting in the way of me loving my son.* I remember telling him, whether he could understand it or not, "Yesterday I really messed up with you and the whole team. I harmed you, hurt you. I didn't handle things correctly. I pray that I won't do anything like that again even though I know I will. I'm really, really sorry." I went on to tell him what I wished I had done.

Simply put, times of helplessness and woundedness that are not resolved from our stories are our unfinished business. Our unfinished business includes whatever bothered us that we still carry around inside us that we are too ashamed to deal with or too ashamed to admit, whatever hurts too much to touch that we can't go there, whatever we react against or are in denial about.

Whatever bothered you growing up that you didn't get healing from; whatever hurt you, harmed you, saddened you, or shocked you; whatever froze inside you that you have not faced and dealt with thoroughly—that is your unfinished business.

Our stories are vital to what we do with our futures. A parent needs to awaken to their own story. If we are not awake to our childhood traumas, wounds, and vows, we will play them out on our children (and in all our significant relationships). All the times we did not have a person to go to with our tears or our jubilation can cause damage. We can form an emotional calcification around our hearts. Going through life alone—even experiencing joy alone—hurts so much that to survive we build walls around our hearts one brick at a time.

That protective hardness begins to form when we promise ourselves that we are not going to let pain happen again. *I'm not going to let that hurt happen again, that sadness, that sorrow. I'm going to be in control instead of being one of those people who get caught crying or laughing. I'm going to get control.* This is the beginning of unfinished business because we are running from being human. The ways in which we lack the courage to face ourselves with compassion become how we treat others—especially those we love the most. We treat them like we treat ourselves.

Lights in the Dark

One of the hardest things about parenting is that we often don't even become aware of our unfinished business until we have played it out on the people we love the most. Our children are often the greatest illuminators of the unfinished business we need to address. There is no way to avoid this, but if we have the ability to admit we were wrong and take responsibility for our actions, we can move to repair much of the damage we have done.

As my (Stephen's) daughter, Emma Claire, began to start the college search process her junior year, I was confronted with a baggage car full of unfinished business. On the outside, I was saying, "You're only seventeen. You have many, many more years to learn about yourself and life. It's okay if you don't know what you want to study right now. Mom and I are here to help you make the best decision you can. And whatever you decide, you can change your mind if you find out it was not the best decision for you." I really meant all that I said. I wanted her to feel the support and freedom she needed to enter the process with as much grace as possible.

However, just below the surface, I was communicating a far different message. "You need to maximize your options. Volunteer. Build your résumé. Study more. Learn an instrument. Write a book. Make a movie." (Yes, I actually suggested in what I thought was a rational way that my seventeen-year-old daughter needed to write, produce, direct, and edit an entire movie.)

On one level, I was saying, "Don't stress. We're here with you." But like a bad voiceover to a foreign language movie, my lips were moving, but they didn't sync with the truth of my heart. "I really need you to make the most of this process and go to an Ivy League school and get a full scholarship." Essentially, I was communicating to her, "You're not doing enough, and who you are is not enough." What I wasn't telling her (or myself) was that I had wished for a parent like me who could have helped me in this scary transition.

As much as I wanted to and as hard as I tried to help her with her college search process, I was blind to the hidden energy I was bringing to our relationship. When Heather and I talked about it one-on-one, I was mostly reasonable, but when we discussed the process as a family, I got crazy. Then one evening after a particularly poor parenting moment with Emma Claire, I said to Heather later in the privacy of our room, "When I was seventeen, if I had had her brain and the support of parents like she does, I would have worked my backside off to get into the best college I could." The combination of hearing my own words and seeing the look on Heather's face woke me up to the unfinished business I was trying to get my daughter's story to fix for me.

I had a different experience when I was in high school. For one, I have a pretty strong case for being diagnosed as ADHD, but when I was growing up, that wasn't even a thing parents and teachers were aware of, let alone equipped to handle. There were no strategies for helping students like me succeed in traditional education environments. The school setting was so difficult for me in middle school and early high school that I secretly thought I had a low IQ. I thought that if I wasn't careful, somebody would find out and I would be exposed—and put in special education classes. Not until my sophomore year in college, when I began taking courses in English and political science (my eventual major and minor), did I begin to see that I could write well and had insight into things my peers sometimes didn't see. And not until graduate school almost a decade later did I discover that in some areas my intellectual capacity is exceptional.

On top of my learning struggles and academic shame, two weeks before my senior year in high school, my parents told my younger sister and me that they were getting a divorce. That event changed the course of my life and destroyed my previous college plans. It was an emotionally stormy time that affected my family's financial security. As the pressure of moving through a divorce mounted, my parents seemed to have little bandwidth to offer consistent emotional or economic support for me in my college search process. I felt like I was alone.

Even though I had done countless hours of therapy to heal concerning that season in my life, the rupture in my family still affected me. As Emma Claire entered into a similar season, residue of that event presented itself in my life like it hadn't in years. As she waded into the college search, my story began to eclipse my best intentions in parenting. It's not that my previous emotional and spiritual work didn't matter, because it did—significantly. Nevertheless, when my daughter turned seventeen and the circumstances of her life resembled mine (even in the slightest ways), I had to deal with my story again. I didn't want her to experience what I had experienced: the feeling of not being supported during a very stressful process. The sad irony is that she got a taste of abandonment, and I was the one who fed it to her.

We can do a lot of growing and healing work in our own personal lives. We can go to workshops, retreats, and recovery meetings. We can read books (like this one) and spend long seasons in individual, couples, and/or family therapy. Many of us need that work and have found that work helpful and rich and redemptive, but it cannot erase our personal histories.

Life is a process that we live daily. We face ourselves. We hopefully learn to celebrate and embrace our gifts. We learn to seek forgiveness and accept our limitations. We grow. We heal. We develop true, intimate relationships with people who encourage us and tell us the truth. And then we move into the next season, and sometimes we need to learn more or to learn the same lessons in a new way. This process of daily living is really the mystery of the recursive grace of God, who invites us more deeply into knowing the mercy that awaits us and the intimacy and love we can experience in the midst of our stories.

A Call to Change

One of the great gifts of having children is the blessing of sanctification. To parent with heart requires that we continue to turn from egocentric patterns of control to face the historic narratives that shape us. Our experiences with our children often tell us more about ourselves than we could teach them. Children are such a gift because they lead us back into our own stories—if we have the courage to see and feel.

Your children are unwittingly inviting you to heal and grow and mature and deepen your understanding of yourself and also your understanding of the grace of God. While we are called to help our children live their stories fully, parenting offers us the opportunity to awaken more deeply to our own stories and the presence of God in our lives.

As parents of young children, Heather and I (Chip) used to stand outside the church nursery waiting for our children to stop crying. Then we'd go to church and wait for the pager to go off. As older parents, we were in a position to volunteer in the nursery and to care for younger, first-time parents who came to drop off their kids. These parents would come in and would be understandably anxious about leaving their children—and the children would be having separation anxiety too. The children would be crying, and the parents would have a list of things they needed us to know. We would listen, smile, and say, "Okay. See you later." Because we knew things would be all right. We knew how to be with crying children, how to hold them, sing songs, and not be anxious. Our experience had taught us that everything would be okay.

Doing something is always easier once we have been through it. The tough part about parenting is that we don't get that chance with our own kids. As parents, we can only learn what our lives are teaching us now. Parenting gives us chances to grow over and over again. We get to listen with new wisdom to the recurring themes for our stories. We stay clumsy like giraffes on ice.

The closer you are to your children, the more blind you are at times to who they really are and what they really need. This is unavoidable. It's almost impossible not to see your own story in the experiences of your children's lives. What's the other option? Keeping your children at arm's distance? Not really attaching well to them? Standing off to the side and being an adviser to their lives? That is worse. There is no win. The closer you get to your children, the more acceptance of clumsiness you have to have.

Understand What You Are Up Against

We will never finish our unfinished business. Parenting with wisdom and integrity mandates that we continue to look at the things we made vows against in our own woundedness, in our own heartache, and in our own traumas and disappointments as children growing up.

We have all made vows against how our hearts are made.

"I will not feel this again."

"I will not need this again."

"I'm not going to depend on anyone again."

"I'm going to be successful."

"No one's ever going to see the real me."

"I've got to be funny."

"I've got to be smart."

"I must be pretty."

To begin to name those vows is to begin to name our unfinished business. Doing so is one of the most courageous things we will ever do and one of the most loving gifts we can give our children.

When we attempt to remove ourselves from how we are made (sensitive, passionate, emotionally needy, desiring, longing beings), we have to make allegiances to other things in order to make our lives work. When we pledge, "I'm not going to be sad," for example, we have to make alliances and bonds with something other than God, caring others, and our honest selves. These pacts end up owning us over time. When we live life in opposition to our stories and how we are made, we push against the past with, "I'll never let that happen again. I can't repeat that." Guess what? If we are pushing against something that hard, that something is the center point in our lives that defines every movement we make. The thing we are against is our reference to everything. It's our god. The demand that life be different for our children than it was for us can become a form of idolatry.

When we press our shoulder against the door of our past, doing so defines the actions of the future. It is a defensive posture. We can't give our children our hearts because our hearts are behind the door. In our attempts to avoid our past wounds, we become prisoners to them. And when we are not free, we are not free to be fully present with our children.

We leave our children with the onerous burden of having to study our masks without knowing our hearts. Because children so need relationship with their parents, they will apply their emotional and spiritual energy to figuring out their parents instead of being free to express their own hearts. They will start to focus on what their parents are feeling, what their parents are thinking, and what their parents need. They will work to make themselves what their parents need. They will begin to parent their parents—and neither the children nor the parents will realize this is happening.

We would all be great parents if we had never been children, because we wouldn't have our own stories of what it means to be a child, what it means to grow up, and what it means to have human parents. But as children, we learn one really important lesson: "If Momma ain't happy, ain't nobody happy." Which is a colloquial way of saying, "It's my job as an eight-year-old to keep these two big grown-ups from acting like children. And when they do, I've got to do what I do best: make them okay."

Admitting the Truth and Learning to Laugh

All of us had human parents, right? Which means they were imperfect. Sometimes the imperfections were glaring. Sometimes parents were horribly abusive and neglectful. Sometimes they abandoned us. Sometimes we were trapped in the grip of addiction with them. And sometimes the imperfections were much less obvious. Sometimes they were selfish. Sometimes they were in bad moods. Sometimes they wanted us to play football or study French or wear a certain outfit to church on Sunday so that they would feel good about themselves and feel as if they were doing something right.

Children can sense this. They know this. And if they aren't free to ask about it, they become confused. Children need to be able to ask questions, and parents need to be able to be emotionally truthful.

One evening I (Chip) was coming home with my son William, and he asked me as I was peering over the steering wheel not talking, "Are you angry?"

Surprised by his question, I quickly said, "No." Then I asked the question to myself and realized I was mad about something that had happened at work. I realized my jaw was fixed, and I could feel a stern look on my face as I focused on what had happened hours earlier. I then said, "William, actually, I am angry about something that happened at work today. But I'm certainly not angry with you." Then we went home.

When a child is free to ask about what they see on their parent's face and the parent is able to tell the appropriate truth to their child, the interaction does several things. It teaches the child to trust themselves. It teaches the child to trust the parent. It helps the child to develop acute empathy. And it releases the child from the burden of raising the parent.

One of the litmus tests for where your unfinished business is showing up is where your children can't laugh at you and you can't laugh at yourself. When you are acting like a buffoon and they are not able to laugh at you, you know you are in a place of unfinished business.

A few weeks ago, I (Stephen) was having a conversation with one of my sons and Heather in the kitchen. We were going round and round, and the conversation was precariously teetering on the verge of a blowup. My son looked me square in the eye and said, "You only listen when you're talking." I turned to Heather and said, "Is that true?" She said, "Yeah, it's kind of true," and we had a big ole laugh about it. His comment still hurt. It still stung. But he was right.

When we have emotionally open and honest relationships with our children, we do a lot of truth telling, a lot of confronting, a lot of making up, a lot of seeking forgiveness, and a lot of laughing. The places they can't laugh with us are the places where we need to grow and heal. There are some stories they know to skirt around. These are the places we have still not surrendered to God, the places about which we have said, "I don't want you there because I don't really trust the story God wrote."

One way to identify your unfinished business is to ask yourself these five courageous questions:

1. What are my ten most painful or shameful life events? (And if you are over eighteen months old, then you have ten.) If you have never made that list, please do. Most people will pretty quickly write down two or three, and then they will get to four or five and will usually say to themselves, "That one didn't hurt that bad." They will judge themselves for putting something on the list. "I

shouldn't be putting that on the list. It's not big enough. Or nobody needs to know."

2. How did each of those events affect me?
3. What vows did I make about those events?
4. What have I had to do to maintain those vows? What are the behaviors I've continued?
5. What has this cost me? What does it cost others?

If you are ready to do the hard work of beginning to name your unfinished business, talk to yourself, to God, or to a wise person or friend about your list. This can be a scary thing to do. If you take the risk, you can find that there are some wise-hearted people who are able to help unburden you if you ask—and God is faithful to be present through it all.

You can't fix what happened. You can't undo it all. However, you can grieve it. You can accept it. You can name it. You can put words to it. You can make amends for it. You can accept responsibility for how your actions have continued to echo in the lives of the ones you love. You can receive forgiveness. You can grow with others, stay in humility, and truly remain in need of God.

This is a great way to begin to deal with unfinished business so that you can show up with your children in life. And you will be able to join with your children when their lives take those same painful turns. Their lives are going to be tragic too. No matter what you do, no matter how good enough of a parent you are, something is going to happen to hurt them.

But you can keep on walking forward with them, even when you are clumsy.

GOING DEEPER

- What vows did you make to make your life work? What vows are keeping you from relationship with yourself, relationship with others, and relationship with God?
- Pay attention for a couple of days to all the "shoulds" you say and hear in your life. If you listen to all the "shoulds" you say to yourself, you will know how you hide your heart from yourself, others, and God.
- What stories do you have to skirt around with your parents? With your spouse? What stories do people have to skirt around with you?

FOUR

This Is Going to Hurt

To love at all is to be vulnerable. Love anything
and your heart will be wrung and possibly
broken. . . . To love is to be vulnerable.

C. S. Lewis

While being a parent means facing our own heartache, it even more awakens us to the depth and breadth of the love that we have inside us for our children. Love for our children amplifies our longings for goodness, home, beauty, and the hope for a future that is stamped in our hearts. This love awakens us to finding glory in the smallest moments as experienced in the lives of our children. A delighted smile. First steps. An out-of-sync dance recital. An excited face on Christmas morning. Catching lightning bugs. The love in our hearts for our children opens us up to levels of wonder and awe to which we had previously been oblivious.

With this depth of joy in love, we also open our hearts to greater pain. When we dare to love someone so deeply, we are assured that our hearts will be broken more times than we can count and filled to the brim more than we can stand. There is nothing more burdensome and beautiful than parenting, nothing more simultaneously full of opportunities to renew hope and occasions for great sorrow. Truth be told, when we enter parenting, we have signed a lifetime contract of love—even a covenant of love. A covenant has no out clause, no "I'm done with this experiment." Once a parent, always a parent. There is no out, and yet there is a lifetime of walking forward toward where love calls us.

So much beauty and joy and wonder and gratitude come with this covenant. And yet, again, also pain. We need to be able to walk through pain and treasure joy to live the covenant. We must learn how to find healing in our hurt, grow through our failures, celebrate the milestones, and have gratitude in life's daily ups and downs. We must have a wide bandwidth for grief and for joy so that our children have a place to come as their lives happen. We have to be good enough at dealing with pain in productive ways to raise our children and good enough at hoping to help them grow their own dreams.

One of the greatest and most difficult things we could ever do is become parents. When we become parents, we are guaranteed that our lives will become more painful than we hoped and less in control than we ever would have planned. As one parent said, "When I had kids, it was like someone took my heart out and now it's out there walking around in the world without me."

If we don't do the experience of hurt well and we don't do grief well, we cannot do joy well, because they all are a part of the burden of love. If we want our children to love joy and to laugh and find the beauty in sunsets and the magic in frogs and tadpoles, we have to have room in our hearts for all of life's experiences. If we do hurt well and can enter into the pain of life with them—the stuff that's not their fault and the stuff that's not our fault as well as the stuff that is their fault and the stuff that is our fault—then we will be able to do a lot of joy well, a lot of celebration well.

It's impossible for all the wants and desires we have for our children to be met. There are many blessings in being a parent, but one of the richest, most life-altering blessings isn't the momentary blessing of a good outcome or a hope fulfilled; it's the holy blessing of being called to face life on life's terms and persevere through it all. Because life hurts, we need to be able to face the hurt in three particular ways: grief, struggle, and regret.

Grief

It was a beautiful spring night in early April. The trees were budding. The days were getting warmer, but the nights were still cool. Heather and Emma Claire were at a movie. I (Stephen) was bowling with our youngest sons, Henry and Teddy. Elijah was off at a friend's house for a birthday party. We had just finished our first frame when my phone rang. It was the kind of call you never want to get. Heather was on the other end. She had a serious and panicked tone in her voice. "Stephen, they've taken Elijah to the hospital. He fell in a fire pit. Meet us there."

Heather and I separately raced to the hospital from different sides of town. She arrived just before I did. I made my way into the back of the emergency room and into the cramped trauma bay to find my son surrounded by a team of doctors and nurses. It was terrible. He was in horrendous pain, and there was nothing Heather or I could do to give him relief. Tragically, that was the easy part, because the next two weeks in the burn unit took all of us to places we never planned to go.

When a person gets a burn, it's not just the burn that hurts. The recovery is worse. The skin graft donor sites bring the most excruciating pain. A human skin graft is basically human sod off one part of the body transplanted to another part that needs to grow new skin. So my son had a quadrant of flesh taken off his thigh. I'll spare all the traumatic details of recovery, but several days later, once he was strong enough, the physical therapy started.

The physical therapist told Elijah that he needed to be able to walk two laps around the burn unit before he could go home. Because of the pain on the donor site, he could barely walk two feet. Two laps might as well have been a marathon. The first day of rehab he walked just a few doors down the hall. The second day he made one lap. His face told us the full story. There was nothing we could do to help him except encourage him and be present literally every step of the way.

After one particularly painful procedure, he broke; it was one of many times. And because he was raised in a home where he could have heart, through his tears he was able to ask questions such as "Why is God letting this happen to me? Why doesn't God protect me? Daddy, why did you let those doctors take me into that room by myself when you said you wouldn't?" He was able to cry out in his pain, and we were utterly powerless to do anything—except to stay.

A few days later, he made five laps. He had to dig deep within himself and push himself. Watching him fight through the pain to make those laps was inspiring. He was heroic. Heather and I stayed with him through it all. Friends came, and we prayed. We took turns sleeping by his side. Full recovery took a long time and included physical healing and many sleepless nights of night terrors.

This was a life-altering event for our entire family. The physical trauma was significant, but more so were the emotional scars created. The experience was terrible for him. It was terrible for us because we love him so much.

He paid a price to find that strength within himself—to push himself so he could go home. The cost was the loss of his own innocence. His belief that the world was good was shattered (though he still believes there is goodness in the world). Elijah is not a melancholy person. He loves to laugh. Now, years later, we are closer as a family because we faced the fear and the hurt of the trauma and stayed in the struggle with him.

We also got through this because we let others love us in the midst of it. The people who loved us, and were with us, and came and sat in the hospital room all night with us, and brought us ice cream, and prayed with us, and continued to care for us as we cared for him for many months made it possible for us to persevere. Still today on the anniversary of the event, people send texts because they remember. People still care. We got through it, broken hearts and all, because we are known well by others.

A huge component of perseverance in grief is having people know us, encourage us, and stay with us in the midst of our grief. People loved us in the midst of our story so that we could love Elijah. We were forced to let the events of this season shape his life in ways we would not have wanted, would not have hoped, and could not have prepared for.

When tragedy strikes, our ability to stay with our children in it, as opposed to creating a world in which no grief exists—no loss, no pain, no hurt—is the difference maker. To have this ability, we have to be really good at living from our own hearts—really adept at recognizing our own feelings. We also need the support of many people to encourage our hearts in the process. No human is made to do life alone. We need others and God.

The idea that it takes a village to raise a child is true, but it really takes a whole platoon of other like-hearted people, because the thing that gets us through the struggle is people who know what struggle is too. As parents, we need other grown-ups to whom we can tell the truth in our pain of how hard it can be—even on a good day. We need others to celebrate the joys when they come, because they come too.

Children need to know that their parents are capable of living fully (in celebration and grief and everything in between). When this happens, children become experienced in using the emotional and spiritual tools that allow them to keep heart. A child who is allowed and helped to experience grief, and supported and affirmed in celebration, is a child who is developing the tools they need to live fully.

Parents spend a lot of life putting children in the right private school, making sure they go to the right youth group, and helping them do the right things—all of which is good. However, if the agenda is to establish a setting that is really about protecting the parents from having to struggle, then the parents' actions are not really benefitting the children.

We mistakenly believe that if we give our children the *best* things, they will have the *best* lives. We need to ask ourselves as parents, "Do I want my children to be full-hearted people, or do I want them to be a success in the eyes of the world?" These don't necessarily go hand in hand.

Parenting corners us with a reality that life is less than what we can dream. If we dare love our children fully, parenting disarms us of our control and certainty. We are left to face life on life's terms: life is wonderful, and it is going to hurt. This is our struggle.

Struggle

The deep human experience is struggle. It's not success. This is certainly true for parenting. We can't win at parenting. To parent with heart is to learn to struggle well. While there are some obvious struggles with our children, spouses, and others, the real struggle in parenting is with ourselves (and with God).

Humans are born knowing how to struggle. We are designed for it. Children are great at struggling. Just look at the first moments of birth. What does a baby have to do to get out of the womb? Struggle. And when it starts to make a noise for the first time, it's not a coo; it's a scream. Then the baby reaches and grasps and sucks and fights and wants to live. It struggles. Have you ever watched kids play? They're all in, and when the blocks fall over, they might cry for a second, but then they go right back to stacking up the blocks.

There are four realities most of us don't necessarily like but we must learn how to struggle with if we are going to live fully and parent well.

1. *The best we ever become is clumsy.* We are always going to be living within a context of imperfection. To live well and to parent well is to live into the paradox of getting really skilled at being clumsy. Even doctors are practicing medicine—they open up a patient for surgery and hope it goes well.

2. *We are WIPs (works in progress).* No matter how high we climb on the sand mountain of perfection, we are not going to reach the top. And even if we could reach the top, we can't stay. We will always be works in progress. We are going to mess up, forget something, or ignore something. We will bump into things or not know something as we press on, dreaming and hoping and living. We are created to continually learn and grow.

3. *We know less than we can learn.* Life is unpredictable. God can seem so obscure. We are never going to have all the answers. We are always going to have questions. It takes a lifetime to learn how to live. We are not going to figure it all out. Often it takes the first half of life to figure out that we can't figure it out. This doesn't mean we stop living; it means we get better at asking questions.

4. *Life is tragic, and God is faithful.* The terms of our human existence are anchored in this truth. This is our fundamental tension. Learning how to struggle well reconciles these two things. How we engage this tension and how we let this tension do its work in us have great significance for how we parent.

This fourth reality is the cornerstone of life and faith and love. It's hard to deny (though many try to) the tragedy of life. How can life be tragic and God be faithful? Appreciating this mystery requires looking a little deeper.

In the ancient Hebrew world, the word for faithful (*emeth*) meant "reliability, stability, or firmness." The Hebrews were born into truth. It wasn't something they had to discover or figure out. God is I AM—the origin of all and the end of all. The Hebrews knew that God is the truth. But they had a problem. They saw reality and said, "You know, God, you're the truth. You're the constant. You do not change. But when I look around, reality tells a different story. Reality has despair and destruction and divorce and darkness and death—plus a few pestilences and plagues. Nothing seems permanent. This reality is a mess." They had a conflict and a struggle. God is faithful, and life is tragic.

Life is so tragic that it causes us to ask tough questions such as, Is God good? Is God even present? Does God really care? Am I alone? Am I known? Am I loved?

A great story of a person dealing with the struggle of these four realities is the story of Jacob in the book of Genesis. Jacob, whose name means "to deceive," was deceiving himself and others and thought he could deceive God. He was always cutting a deal. He was always trying to manage life to get the upper hand and come out ahead. He was always trying to figure out how to come out on top. He did this to the point that he sacrificed everything around him to manipulate and to have his own way.

The last deal he cut left him alone in the desert. That night the Man showed up, and they fought. They struggled all night long. At the end of the struggle, Jacob got a blessing. He got a blessing for fighting. He got a blessing for showing up emotionally and spiritually and wrestling with the being of God. He got a blessing even while trying to keep his false identity, trying to have his way, trying to have control, and still have a life. In the end, he lost his ego and gained himself.

His hip was snapped, and his name was changed. He was broken of his perfectionism and control. He moved from being a survivor to becoming a full-hearted person. God blessed him with a new name, Israel, which means "to struggle with God and live"—to struggle with God and in doing so find his life. From then on, with every step he took, he walked with a limp that reminded him of being human.

The name Israel is an offer for all of us. Only in our ability to struggle can we begin to reconcile the conflict between love and tragedy. Like Jacob, we need to face the struggle with ourselves and with God, receive our blessing, and walk in faith (limp). Struggling well is a threshold into a new life in which we become really good at being human and therefore have a great opportunity to become a good-enough parent.

In the midst of the struggle of life, God is telling a story of love. God is creating something in the midst of the tragedy. The tragedy doesn't take away the faithfulness of God or the fruitfulness of our lives. God is re-creating over and over again, but we have to surrender to the re-creation in our own stories in order to trust that our children's stories are likewise unfolding. Otherwise we will try to pad their rooms so they don't get bruises or turn our heads so we don't have to watch.

If we haven't experienced some re-creation in our own stories as parents, then we won't let our children risk their hearts. On the other hand, if we are willing to accept that life is tragic, then we can walk through the tragedy with our children. We can help them face it instead of trying to keep them from it.

Regret

Because we love our children, and because we want good for them, and because we are imperfect, we are going to have regrets. Along with the grief of life and the struggle with ourselves and with God, regrets are a part of raising children. It's impossible for our children's lives to meet the depth of our dreams and desires for them. Regret is one of the greatest testimonies that we love our children.

I (Chip) am older now, and therefore I know more regret. Regret is not a bad thing, really. Regret is a testimony of grasping love because in it is a wish that we had done things or could have done things differently. I know and have experienced what we write in this book. Our family has been through multiple surgeries, deep heartaches, cancer, great joys, sweet mercies, deep struggles, ups and downs, warps and woofs. And we have had the great enjoyment of having persevered through it all together. We have lived together; we have struggled together.

One day soon after Sonya and I and our sons had moved to Murfreesboro, our youngest son, William, who was five at the time, spent some time with his aunt while I was doing some errands. When I picked him up, she reported that William had been disrespectful.

William was then and still is quite the truth teller. As he and I pulled out of the driveway on our way home, I said, "William, why didn't you mind your aunt?" It was the first thing out of my mouth.

He said, "I don't know." I asked again, and again he came up with the same answer, what I judged to be an excuse.

As we turned onto our street, I said, "William, I'm going to give you the time it takes to get to the end of the street to give me an answer." (Not my best parenting moment.) He couldn't even see over the dashboard to see the end of the street. I thought I was parenting. We headed to the end of the street and his doom.

Out of the blue, he asked me what eight times eight is. I looked at him. His forehead looked a little wrinkled with thought, and his eyes seemed genuinely curious. But I thought I knew what he was really up to. He was trying to throw me off the scent so that I wouldn't stay on track and he wouldn't face the consequences of his misbehavior.

I kind of wisely smiled and answered the simple multiplication question. "Sixty-four." Then I turned back to the straight and narrow, the topic at hand. "William, what's the answer to my question?"

He said after a few seconds of staring at the dash, as I came to the end of the street, "What's sixty-four times sixty-four?"

How did he know my Achilles' heel, the place of absolute struggle and defeat? Math. I looked at William, applied the brakes to come to a stop, and said, a little exasperated, "William, I don't know."

To which he quickly responded, "And I don't either."

I saw in that moment the graciousness, trust, and pure-heartedness of this precious child who had told me the truth the first time I had asked: "I don't know." In the face of getting in trouble, not even being able to see the end of the street, he stuck with love, believing that my question must be good because I, Dad, was asking it and that somehow Dad just didn't understand. He gave me mercy, and in his vulnerable and trusting love, he gave me grace. I remember the incident years later, am thankful for it, and still regret it.

More than twenty years later, we were talking one evening, and William said, "You know, Dad, Mom, we hung out together all the time. We went on vacation, and I had this idea that you really liked going with us." He paused. "And then it finally hit me. It seems like we had more struggles than other families. I see now it was because we were together."

I laughed because it was so true! We were together, and because we were together, all that comes with being in relationship came with us. We argued, talked, cried, disagreed, struggled, and celebrated, and when they left home, we took the time to remember as we said good-bye to a huge portion of our lives. I remember how William cried when he told his brother good-bye as Tennyson left for college, not because he would never see him but because life was to change again, so we honored the reality of it.

William was right. We lived together, so we got to make more mistakes with one another. The more mistakes we make with the ones we love, the more regret we have. If we love somebody deeply, we are going to miss them when they're gone. If we love somebody deeply, we are going to harm them too.

To have sadness and regret about your past with your children means you care. The sadness tells you that you value what you no longer have. If your kids are out of diapers, look at some pictures of them from years ago. You can't get that time back. It's gone. If that is sad to you, then you know you were there and someone and/or something mattered to you.

Regret works in a similar way. Regret says we recognize the missed opportunities and the mistakes we made. This is a good thing—especially if we don't let the mistakes define us as parents. Regret lets us know how to take responsibility for who we were. What irony that the task of parenting is assigned to people who generally lack the wisdom to do it well and that only through experiencing life do we see how we could have done things differently.

When all is said and done, we need to be good-enough parents. Becoming a good-enough parent really means being good at being human. The desire to be known by others and our children is a movement away from performance and a movement toward presence. A full-hearted parent, in other words, is someone who can tolerate the pain of relationship and regret. It's a person who can stay human (imperfect and clumsy) and let their children remain human too. It's through intimacy that we find fulfillment. As human beings, we are only fully alive when we are living fully in relationship with ourselves, others, and God. We can follow all the recipes, but if we are not able to grieve, struggle, and face regret, we cannot have love, intimacy, and trust.

GOING DEEPER

- Spend some time making a list of when you have defended yourself against the inevitable pain of life by not letting yourself be fully present to experience the joy of a beautiful moment. Close your eyes and try to picture each item on the list. Imagine how those moments could have felt, and then draw a picture, write a poem, take a photograph—do something that expresses that joy to you.

- Regrets. Frank Sinatra can't be the only one who's had a few. Take a moment to consider your regrets, particularly in regard to your children. Write a letter to them. (You don't have to send it or give it to them. Just make a start!) It is never too late to make amends, to ask for forgiveness, to open yourself up to being different. Doing so matters to those you love and who love you.
- Tell your children at least three things you love or appreciate about them that you haven't told them before. Tell family stories at the dinner table. "Remember when . . ." is a great way to begin. One way to remind yourself that the pain and stress of parenting are worth it is to recall all the blessings that come with the roles of mom and dad.

FIVE

Failure Is Not Optional— It's Inevitable

Success is not final, failure is not fatal: it is the courage to continue that counts.

Winston Churchill

When my (Chip's) son Tennyson was born, Sonya had a distressful delivery. As soon as he was born, they took him straight to the nursery so that she could be attended to. When I finally made it to the nursery, I remember peering through the window and looking at my son. I had not gotten to hold him yet, nor had Sonya. He was so small. I remember he lifted up his head and turned it and put it down. Standing there after all the stress and struggle we had just been through, I was overcome, and tears streamed down my face. Looking through the window, I made promise after promise. "I will never allow you to be harmed. I will always look out for you. I will always be there for you." The list went on and on, and I meant every word.

By the time we got home from the hospital with Tennyson, I had already begun to move away from the promises in one way or another. I had made promises that only God can fulfill. It's not that I was wrong or foolish for making those promises. They were pure expressions from a father who was deeply committed to loving his son. But they were made before I really accepted a fundamental emotional and spiritual truth: life on life's terms means that I will fail—often. The larger our desire to love our children, the more failure we will have to face.

I remember when one of our sons was in middle school. Sonya and I wanted him to participate in a country-wide leadership program. We pushed him to be a part of it. Many of the "right" kids were doing it, and we didn't want him to miss out on an opportunity to build his future résumé. He told us several times that he didn't want to do it. We believed his not wanting to participate was due to his immaturity. We continued to press, and he continued to protest. Finally, he said, "I'll just fail the interview." He did not get into the leadership program. I am certain he convinced the interviewer of his disinterest. And the interviewer actually listened—unlike his parents. Afterward I remember saying, "I think he didn't want to do it." I remember thinking what an opportunity he missed, and at the same time, he is not the kind of person who wants to participate in things like that. God has written other desires on his heart. Because we thought we knew so much, we didn't listen to him. Our desires for him kept us from listening to him and paying attention to how he is made.

This was not the only time an interaction like this occurred between the two of us. Years later, I remember him saying, "Dad, do you want to hear what I have to say, or do you just want to tell me what to think. I'd rather make my own mistakes than try to do what *you* think is best." In that moment, I saw again how I needed to change. I've continued to work on paying attention to what he says as opposed to paying attention to what I want him to do. In my desire to want what I thought was best for him, I put our relationship at risk. Many parents, in the name of progress for their children, miss out on relationship with them.

This doesn't mean we never ask our kids to do things they don't want to do. It means we need to attend to what they are telling us about themselves and who God made them to be. We must continue to remember that we are in relationship with them. They are not blank slates on which we write their best lives.

When we are able to see and accept our failures and mistakes, we have the incredible opportunity to continue to grow with our children. When we as parents let go of our selfish desire to be great, we quit performing and discover more freedom to be our truer selves with our children. We are not in some kind of parenting contest. There is no podium, and we will not get a gold medal.

When we live in the paradox that failure and grace are inextricably linked, we tumble down off the sand mountain of perfection and start living on the ground as human beings with other human beings—parent with child.

The book of Matthew in the New Testament contains an account of Jesus saying a version of the same thing. He was asked a very "sand mountain" kind of question by his disciples: "Who gets the highest rank in God's kingdom?" (18:1 Message). If Jesus had been leading a parenting seminar, the question would have been, "How do I become the best parent?"

> He called a little child to him, and placed the child among them. And he said: "Truly I tell you, unless you change and become like little children, you will never enter the kingdom of heaven. Therefore, whoever takes the lowly position of this child is the greatest in the kingdom of heaven. And whoever welcomes one such child in my name welcomes me." (Matt. 18:2–5)

He said this to his disciples—those who were closest to him and knew him intimately. They had seen Jesus perform miraculous feats. They had seen him heal sick people. They had heard Jesus's message daily, a message of love, humility, powerlessness, surrender, and courage. A few of them—his closest friends, Peter, James, and John—had been to a mountain where Jesus showed them his full glory (the transfiguration) and where they saw Elijah and Moses and heard the voice of God express delight in Jesus. Even after all this, they still didn't fully grasp the core themes in Jesus's message (his Good News). Doing your best and being good isn't the point; you can't save yourself (or your children) from the mess you are in. That's not your job.

Like all of us, the disciples wanted their emotional and spiritual security to come from their success. "Tell me how to be the best, and I'll try to do it. Give me the five tasks to living well so I can know I'm doing a good job." They, like us, were invested in a way of being that was rooted in toxic shame and fear—a system that demands performance over presence. This conflict shows up in parenting all the time. As parents, we want approval more than we want relationship.

Jesus turned the tables on that system (literally), and in this passage from the book of Matthew, he made his point clear. Children live more truthfully than adults. We need to surrender to being changed and allow God to bring us back to who we are created to become. If we want to find the freedom and the fullness of life we are made to experience, we must follow the example that Jesus gave. We are called to live in childlike dependence and faith.

Power versus Presence

As parents, we have a significant role in nurturing, guiding, instructing, and disciplining our children, but our authority and responsibility as parents come only from the fact that we were born first, have more experience, and hopefully have more wisdom. We don't have to pass a test to become a parent. Our children don't expect perfection from us. They need us to be humans with them. The basis of being fully human is retaining the humility of neediness with which all children come into this life.

Too often we live in power struggles with our children. Most often these struggles come from within us. We are in a bind between how our agendas for our children conflict with our children's agendas. And on a deeper level, we are also in conflict with how our agendas for our children conflict with the stories God is writing in our lives and in the lives of our children. We live in a pair of double binds: (1) the children we have do not always act like the children we want, and (2) the God who is does not always act like the god we want.

Instead of dealing with these deeper issues of the heart, we too often force our agendas to attempt to make our anxieties go away. That becomes "My will be done." We exert power. We do this overtly by force, covertly by manipulation, or passively by withdrawal or neglect. An opposite thing can also happen. Sometimes we succumb to our fear of our children's pain and disappointment and abdicate our responsibilities. We appease our children, give in to them, or pacify them. We effectively let our children's moods or situations hold us emotionally hostage. When we don't know what to do, we make them the decision makers and indulge our children to keep them from grief, struggle, and regret.

All parents do versions of both of these things. We are human. Usually, the impulse to control or be controlled by our children does not come from some sinister place within us. It most often comes from a place of unrecognized fear. When our wills conflict with the wills of our children (or God's will), we have only three options:

1. Exert power
2. Give in
3. Recognize what is happening, sidestep the power struggle, and engage our hearts and our children's hearts with wisdom, strength, tenderness, and authenticity

By no means are we saying that every moment of conflict with our children is some deep, intra-psychic struggle. All people are selfish and want their own way. (To be different is a choice and takes practice.) Nor are we saying that every moment of parenting turns into this counseling-type process. Very often no means no. Frequently, time-outs, restrictions, and discipline are our first and best moves. What we are saying is that on an emotional, spiritual, and psychological level, much of what our children are doing is asking us questions: "Is your heart big enough, deep enough, mature enough, and wise enough to stay with me? Will you love me well?"

Author and teacher Dan Allender talks about the four characteristics of love. These are essential to parenting (and any significant relationship).[1]

1. *Delight in the presence of the other.* Are we able to celebrate and receive the wonder and beauty of our children? (Most of us do this really well as parents until our children hit middle school.) Are we able to see more good than bad in them and still see the truth of who they are?

2. *Curiosity about the heart of the other.* As parents, are we willing to try to understand how our children are uniquely made? Are we willing to step back and look at the work God is doing in their lives and the themes that emerge over time in their stories? Are we able to engage their whole hearts well—even the parts we wish were different?

3. *A willingness to hurt on the other's behalf.* Are we willing to become empathetic enough to imagine what the inner worlds of our children are like? Are we willing to let our hearts break when our children's hearts break? Can we bear their pain?

4. *A willingness to stand in the way of the other.* Another way of saying this is to live with boundaries. Are we willing to consistently stand in the way of their selfishness and engage them in relationship for their good? Children need to know that a presence that is bigger than they are is needed in order for them to be safe. For this to happen, we need to be able to stand firm with care and wisdom and to tolerate their disappointment and displeasure.

Like everything else with parenting, these four hallmarks of love are a daily focus and take a lifetime to live. These hallmarks aren't a checklist as much as guideposts for us in the process of relationship. Our presence as parents blesses or harms our children. The more of our true selves our children are given, the better off they will be. With the blessings comes gratitude, and with the harms comes the need for forgiveness.

Remembering How to Be Childlike

No place does being childlike occur more than in the area of heart expression, which is the language of the child that we can never outgrow. One way to live into Jesus's instruction to "become like a child" is to remember or learn again how to laugh, how to cry, and how to play. This is one of the gifts that children bring to us. They can help us reawaken to the experience of life and being in need again. They can expose us to the kingdom, where we are free of self-conscious criticism—free to be human and free to "let" God be God.

One rainy summer morning I (Stephen) came out into our main living area and saw all four of our children from age seventeen down to twelve building towers with blocks on the dining table. Someone had gotten out our set of blocks from their childhood.

Unlike those of my children, my schedule doesn't change in the summer. I still get up, pray, exercise, shower, dress, grab a protein bar, and head to the office. My head was full of the usual morning thoughts: *I need to get going. Where's my phone? Where's my coffee? What's on my schedule today?*

As I was passing through the kitchen gathering my things, one of them asked me to look at their tower, and something occurred to me: "Oh, we can play together." I put down my keys and phone and satchel and started building my own tower. As often happens in our family, the activity turned into a bit of a playful competition among the four of us guys because that's what guys do, right? We were videotaping one another's towers and bumping the table on purpose to mess with one another. And then after a few minutes, we all stood back to admire our towers and brag and trash-talk. But while we were doing our thing, my daughter was being herself—quietly being marvelous at the other end of the table. I looked over, and she was standing on a chair placing the final block on her tower. It reached all the way to the ceiling. We all froze in amazement. While we were all being boys at one end of the table, she was being herself. And she was beautiful. We all just admired her. Then we had eggs and coffee and moved on to the rest of the day. What happened was nothing extraordinary, but it was beautiful. We were just being together, playing.

I don't know if they will remember that moment. I don't know if they're going to say years from now, "Hey, Dad, remember that morning when we played blocks together when we were teenagers, and you stayed home from work and had coffee and we built things?" I hope they do. I know I will because in that moment I was aware that I was off the sand mountain and on the ice with them, and we were all experiencing life together. That is what presence is all about. We need to drink these moments in, mark them, and remember them. They are antidotes for our failures and balms for our regrets.

The Paradox of Failure and Forgiveness

Our best parenting moments aren't when we think they are; they are when we are being ourselves—and we are no less ourselves than when we mess things up. One of the great paradoxes we must come to accept is that we often grow closer to our children in our failures and in their heartaches. One of the hardest things about life is accepting that we can't fix the pain we cause other people. They cannot fix the pain they cause us. That is the basis of forgiveness. "I recognize I've harmed you, and I can't fix the pain or repair the damage adequately." Or, "You have caused this pain in me, and you don't have the power to heal me."

The parent who can see when they fail is in a parent-child relationship that bestows hope. That is the irony. Our sorrow, recognized and handled responsibly, is a statement of our unending love for our children and our hope for our children. If we can't recognize "I'm doing harm," our children are hopeless with us. Healthy parents seek forgiveness. Unhealthy parents seek justification. They say the words "I'm sorry, but . . ." They subtly become victims and their children their perpetrators. They are demanding their children be responsible for the parents' feelings.

"I'm sorry I yelled at you for being late, *but* you should've called."

"That was really lousy the way I gave you the cold shoulder when I got upset, *but* when you act like that, what am I supposed to do?"

"Forgive me for overreacting when you let the dog walk on the rug with muddy paws, *but* that rug cost a fortune."

The Power of Forgiveness

Refusing to be humble and take responsibility for our own actions and reactions is reflected in the statement "They did the best they could." So many people avoid their own inner lives by saying, "My parents did the best they could." They use that phrase to justify their parents' actions. They offer a cheap forgiveness in an attempt to let themselves off the hook. "My parents did the best they could, so I'm doing the same thing. I'm doing the best I can."

Let's be frank. We need to be really good at seeking forgiveness as a humble form of living. Any of our efforts to love well rise and fall like the tide.

I (Chip) remember a wonderful physician who came for treatment some years ago. J. T. was a physician of international recognition and a former head of a specialty at a well-known academic hospital. J. T.'s wife had died eight years previously of cancer. She had been abandoned, along with their children, due to his profession and his alcoholism.

J. T. had always planned to cut back and come home, but he had not planned to do so because his spouse had cancer.

He took a sabbatical from work for nine months while his wife was sick. He had peace and closeness, turmoil and despair with a woman he had missed for years and years. She had the same with him for nine months as she struggled to live. He had nine months in the family before she died, and afterward his alcoholism took full grip.

The man who sat before me, now sober, had a deep baritone voice and spoke slowly. He possessed strength of character captured behind walls of refusal and years of ignoring his heart. His face bore the marks of age, dignity, and loss, like nature's cuttings in limestone.

I asked him to tell me about one of his sons when he was young. He told a story that spoke of the promises he once had made and the wishes in his heart. I asked J. T. what he used to call his son when he was little. J. T. said, "I called him Johnny." So I asked him to write a short letter to Johnny, and I gave him the first sentence:

Dear Johnny,
  Every time I think about you I want to say . . .

I invited J. T. to return to his heart and remember how much he loved his son. He slowly said, "I want to say, 'I love you, Johnny.'" J. T. breathed in against a sharp pain, held his breath for a moment, and then exhaled, opening a flood of tears that ran down the crevices of his tired face. He wept and shook with his head bowed in sorrow, contempt, and regret. He saw and felt a piece of the life he had missed, which opened the doorway to healing.

I told him to finish the letter and I would invite his son to treatment so he could tell Johnny the truth. Then J. T.

said, "Please, no," shaking his bowed head back and forth. "I can't, I can't," he moaned.

I said, "What do you mean? Don't miss this opportunity. What would stop you?"

He leaned forward a bit and then raised his head. He breathed out heavily as he said in agony, "He will think I'm weak." The words conveyed agonizing despair as his tears continued. J. T. had never heard the words "I love you" himself, and he had not uttered them. He had tried to earn them, and in doing so, he had forgotten his heart and lost his way.

J. T. would be restored by facing what his heart had rejected and missed and what his son had missed and might now reject. I asked J. T. if he was willing to take the risk. A week later, his fifty-four-year-old son arrived to hear three words that a world-renowned, brilliant, powerful healer had never uttered. This time J. T. would offer himself to life, to God, and to his son.

Johnny sat in the office across from his father as J. T. read a piece of the letter. When he read the words "I love you" to his son, J. T. wept in brokenness.

Johnny sat still for a long moment, then leaned forward with his hands holding on to the arms of the chair. With controlled vitriol, he said, "You're too late. I needed that then. I'm grown." Silence filled the room for a moment.

J. T. said, "I know," and looked down in tears.

Then with pained anger, the son said, "Didn't you know I needed you?" With anguish on his face, he asked, "Didn't you know?" He looked out the window for a moment before years of tears started for him. Johnny hated them as he looked at his father.

"I'm sorry," J. T. said. "I love you, Johnny. I'm sorry."

PARENTING *with* HEART

Johnny both hated and loved his walls being breached. Then he said, "But Dad . . ." Both men sat bowed in their grief. Then the old man stood, and the son rose to fall into his arms.

Love that is born in surrender and forgiveness opens the door for God to heal the past and start a future.

Unless we admit our failures, grow in love, and live in dependence, we can't become who we are made to be, and we miss what we are made to do. Then our children miss the blessing of our presence. Jesus said, "Unless you change and become like little children, you will never enter the kingdom of heaven" (Matt. 18:3).

Johnny tasted a piece of heavenly bread handed to him by his own dad. The mark of an emotionally and spiritually healthy person is the willingness to seek forgiveness. Healthy parents seek forgiveness. They say, "I am sorry." Period.

We need to live in the practice of giving and receiving forgiveness. We need to do so especially as parents, because there is only a rare day that goes by that we don't hurt our children or that our children don't hurt us.

What Goes Around Comes Around

If we are parents who seek forgiveness, then we can prepare ourselves to receive one of the richest gifts a child can give a parent. We won't discover one of the marks of being a wholehearted parent until our children are older (at least twenty-four or older). This is when they come and tell us what it was like to be with us—and it wasn't all good. In fact, some of it was harmful and awful. They say, "I was really hurt and scared by some of your parenting."

Often this happens when they get married or have kids. They are thirtysomething, and they say to themselves, "I learned how to treat people like this from my mom. I learned how to be scared of people like this from my dad." They come and visit us a few months or years after getting married and say, "Some crazy stuff happened in our family."

If our kids can come home and do that, and we can bear the weight of it, we have their hearts. If they can tell us about how we failed them, and we can look at them and say, "I'm so sorry. What do you need? What was that like for you? How does it affect your life now?" then and only then will we know that we were a good-enough parent then and are a good-enough parent now. Part of their freedom to be present with us is reflected in their ability to say, "You're a human. You do harm at times." When we give them our hearts, they can give us their hearts later, and we can be reconciled.

Sliding Off the Sand Mountain

So the question we need to be asking as a parent is not "How am I doing?" as in looking for a grade, but "What am I doing?" as in looking toward ourselves to be who our children need. The first question is ego centered. The second question is relationally centered. "How am I doing?" is a sand-mountain question. "What am I doing?" is a relational question, and it leads us to slide about on the ice. This question is really akin to "Who am I?" and "Who are they?" It's far more curious, more open, more humble, more willing, more courageous, and more attractive because it leaves room for others to be themselves with us.

Falling off the mountain sets us free to be interested in the life of another human being. Life is not just about us anymore. We slow down to be interested in the lives of our children, and we discover that they have great things to say, and they surprise us, and we discover again and again that they have incredible ideas about life that they are figuring out for the first time.

Once we accept that failure is not optional, that life is inescapably painful, that we have unfinished business, that we are wired for relationship, and that the best we get is that we are clumsy, we are less ashamed of ourselves. We less often try to undo our pasts through our children. We become increasingly free of the contempt of others. Once we accept that failure is inevitable, we can live on the ice, sometimes skating magnificently free and sometimes having to untangle from a clumsy spill with the people we love.

We become free of our scripts and agendas, and the entire world opens up to us. We become free to accept our limitations and mistakes, victories and celebrations, because our grades no longer define us. Love defines us. We are defined by love and forgiveness, presence and truthfulness. We don't try to pretend that we are someone we're not.

Children with these kinds of parents know they're loved. These parents will stay in the struggle of grief or celebration and live everything else in between. Their parenting is no longer about success and failure but about love and intimacy.

If we have a heart that can face limitations, if we have a heart that can repent, if we have people in our lives who can tell us about us and the impact of us on them, if we can say, "Forgive me," then we are free to be good enough.

We need to plant the roots of our hearts in the things that give life, which means we need to have a willingness to grow by facing our need for forgiveness, help, and guidance. When we do, we become more loving, more joyful, more peaceful, more patient, more kind, more generous, more faithful, more gentle, and more self-controlled. We see the fruit of the Spirit playing out in our lives. And the great thing about fruit is that even rotten fruit that falls from the tree fertilizes the soil. Nothing is wasted in God's spiritual economy. God has the loving ability and the mercy to take our foibles and our failures and our limitations and use them for redemptive purposes in the kingdom. Life isn't up to us—though we get to participate in it with passion. We are free from having to make things turn out okay, and we are free to join in the process of what God is doing.

GOING DEEPER

- Sometimes we make mountains out of molehills. Write down some of the things you make a really big deal out of in your own life with your kids. Make sure to include when you think these are your unfinished business coming into play. Write about the ways these reactions are stealing your joy and robbing you of your delight in your children. Do you need to let some of these go? Or are they worth holding on to? Choose your battles well.

- Consider taking an evening off from "parenting" and spend an hour or two solely delighting in your children. Laugh. A lot.

- This week at dinner ask your children questions about their lives. Try to go beyond the usual surface questions and seek to really hear what they are thinking, feeling, dreaming, hoping, and fearing. You don't need answers or solutions or suggestions. You only need to be curious. If this type of thing is new to you, make a list of questions. Asking such questions lets your kids know you care and are trying. Here are some examples to get you started: What do you daydream about? What have your friends been up to? If you could have a shop, what would you sell in it? If you could be a superhero with three powers, what would they be? If you could change your name, what would you change it to?

- How do you manipulate your children so they won't feel? How do you bargain with your children to keep them happy in order to avoid creating new problems for you to deal with?

- When was the last time you felt truly powerless as a parent? How did you respond?

PART TWO

OUT
(Me with You)

SIX

Put On Your Own Mask First

In the unlikely event of an emergency, oxygen
masks will fall from the compartments above.
The bags may not inflate, but oxygen will be
flowing freely. Put on your own mask first
before helping others who need assistance.

every flight attendant

A few years ago, I (Stephen) was invited to travel to Kenya to
be the keynote speaker at a conference for a group of mis-
sionaries from across eastern Africa. Heather and I thought
this would be a great opportunity for our kids to expand
their worldviews, so we decided to make it a family trip. It
was an amazing, once-in-a-lifetime family adventure. It was
a lot of fun and a lot of travel. We made six flights (three
on each end of the trip). Every time we got on the plane,
whether we were in the United States, Europe, or Africa,

the flight attendants would give us the same instructions (sometimes in several languages): "In the unlikely event of an emergency, oxygen masks will fall from the compartments above. The bags may not inflate, but oxygen will be flowing freely. Put on your own mask first before helping others who need assistance."

People hear that warning, but guess what's likely to happen if the plane suddenly loses altitude and those masks drop from the ceiling. Chaos. No one's thinking. Everyone's panicking. Mothers and fathers are likely trying to save their children first, which decreases their own chance of survival. Putting on our own oxygen masks first is one of the wisest and most courageous things we can do for our kids and ourselves—but most parents fail significantly in this area.

As we begin to wake up to the reality that our children need a secure emotional and spiritual foundation for a vibrant, consistent, authentic, and intimate relationship with us, we also wake up to what that means. We as parents have to be really good at taking care of ourselves first. We can't give our children something we don't have. If we don't put on our own oxygen masks first, when stress levels go up we are not going to be able to give our children what they need.

Self-Care Is Courageous

Self-care is difficult for many parents, but it's not logistically as hard as we make it. We are never too busy to care for ourselves, though that is the cliché so many of us use to avoid the struggle for self-care. The real difficulty of self-care is internal. Self-care can be a brave endeavor (especially for moms) when just going to the bathroom when we need to can be a miraculous moment.

The reason why self-care is so courageous for parents is that taking even the briefest moment to put on our own oxygen masks feels like we are taking care of ourselves to the exclusion of others. In reality, we are taking care of ourselves so that we can better care for others. In this way, self-care becomes an act of trust and faith in God. Practicing self-care is a practical way of living in obedience to the sixth commandment: "Remember the Sabbath day by keeping it holy" (Exod. 20:8).

We are made to rest. We are made to reflect. We are made to be renewed. The commandment of Sabbath was given at a time in history when if people did not get up and do hard work, they were likely to make their life more difficult and complicated. And to this God said, "And make sure you take a day when you don't work." That commandment is radical because the fear is "If I don't work today, I might not eat tomorrow." Living in Sabbath is not easy until we trust it as an invitation from God. God asks, "Will you care for yourself a little? Will you rest? Will you let me give to you, replenish you, so you can in turn care for others?"

We are created for rest and play as much as we are created for the work of love. Beyond the obvious physical and psychological refreshment that comes through self-care, the true benefit of incorporating this kind of discipline into our lives as parents is the emotional and spiritual benefit. When we lean into risking self-care, we create the space for dependence on and intimacy with God.

Self-care stops crises of urgency and instigates love. It slows life down. When we as parents put on our own oxygen masks first, we can breathe. Our breathing will allow us to be conscious and present to what is going on around us. It enables us to be responsible and wise instead of reactive. As parents who are present, we can turn to face our children in *their* chaos and provide them with security and care. When we are not running on empty, we have more to give our children.

As powerful, holy, and essential as self-care is, not practicing it is just as dangerous. When we as parents perpetuate our illusions of control, deny our created design, and ignore our needs for replenishment, we exclude ourselves from the full benefits of the presence of God in our lives—not to mention our full presence in our children's lives. As parents, most of our chaos is internal. We are great at looking a certain way and yet feeling another way. Our hearts are divided. We are great at appearance rather than being who we really are. We overfunction on the shifting sands of anxiety, and it's not sustainable. Our attempts at control demand our full attention. Ironically, in the name of loving our children, we can end up emotionally abandoning them when we are exhausted, stressed out, and preoccupied.

What the flight attendants don't say when they are reminding us to put on our own masks first is "If you don't, you are both going to die." Too often so much of parenting is done from a posture of "I'm going to give to my children first and give to myself last." This is understandable and sounds sacrificial on the surface. It can seem very loving. It also can be a very self-centered style of parenting.

Often we give to our children first so we can feel like a certain kind of parent. We parent as if we are trying to earn something or prove something. We live and parent from a point of view that says we have to work really hard before we can take a break, before we get to rest. "Only if I work hard and do more do I deserve a break." When we parent in this way, our parenting can become mechanical and reactive. We get our children taken care of instead of caring for our children. At the end of the day, we are exhausted. We don't want our children to remember us as reactive parents, nor do we want them to see themselves as burdens.

The truth is if we care for ourselves well, then our efforts at giving are really heartfelt, genuine, and engaging. The longer we go without restoration and replenishment, the less authentic and loving our parenting becomes. Sadly, too many parents won't take responsibility for their own well-being, and they end up not giving their best. They end up ordering their lives around tasks and merely surviving instead of thriving.

Knowing When to Stop

When we go for periods of time without practicing wise self-care, we are apt to revert to our childhood survival strategies. Many parents don't recognize their need for self-care until they've waited too long. They fall into their beds night after night with nothing left to offer. They explode in rage when their prescribed daily order is disrupted. They collapse in tears in sheer exhaustion.

Knowing when we need to reset is fundamental to beginning to care for ourselves—and essential to full-heartedly loving our children. A simple acronym can help us spot areas of need: HALT.

Hungry

Anxious

Lonely

Tired

When we don't heed HALT, we literally begin operating out of our brain stem (sometimes called the reptilian brain). The more we act out of that place, the more reactive and primal we become. When we aren't nourished (hungry), addressing our neediness (anxious), connected in relationship (lonely), and rested (tired), we can't help but go into self-preservation mode.

When we get "hangry," as some people call the combination of hunger and anger, our bodies perceive distress, our blood sugar starts to drop, and we feel we might, as one parent quipped, "eat one of my children if they have salsa on them." When we don't attend to our anxiety, which is a basic recognition of unaddressed fears, we tend to over-control or give in to rage. We end up treating people as problems. When we are lonely and not getting our needs met from other grown-ups, we will expect our children to meet us in a relationship that is above their pay grade. When we are tired and not getting enough rest, we end up making rash decisions and reacting to our emotions instead of addressing them.

If we don't pay attention to HALT, we are likely to act out or act in. We act out by raging, pouting, or blaming. We act in by withdrawing, fantasizing, or becoming depressed. When we act out and/or act in, we are attempting to get our legitimate needs met in illegitimate ways. When we recognize

HALT, we can begin to care for ourselves in legitimate, re-storative ways.

One Size Doesn't Fit All

What we need in terms of self-care is different in different seasons of our lives. Having young children, having older children, or having children who have moved out often influences what we need and how we can get our needs met. There is not a one-size-fits-all formula. Becoming a good-enough parent means becoming flexible enough, mature enough, and responsive enough to adapt as we and our families change. As life continues to change, we change with it. We keep growing as our children are growing.

Without self-care, we have a more self-centered, irritable, shortsighted way of managing people. (This principle also works in marriage and at work.) Putting on our own oxygen masks first is really important. Doing so means we have gotten to know ourselves well enough to know what works for us.

Self-care can seem so difficult that if we don't practice it and commit to it, then it will not happen. All the demands that come our way seem so crucial but rarely are. To practice self-care, we begin by setting up and maintaining rhythms, rituals, and practices that are uniquely our own. To do self-care well, we find what works for us and gives us the oxygen we need. What restores your heart? What works for one person doesn't always work for another.

If we are not restored, we have nothing to offer. There is a truth about us humans: we are a little bit like trees—we have to be fed. The primary food we need to have is spiritual and emotional restoration, replenishment, redemption, and re-creation, and the only way we know our needs is by knowing our limits. We have to know our limits to have a great life.

By knowing and maintaining our limits, we have more to offer the people we love. We cannot give what we do not have. Putting on our own oxygen masks first is counterintuitive when life is stressful. But when we have something to offer, the ones we care about the most can receive emotional and spiritual food from us. Children feed off their parents. For their sake, we have to take care of ourselves.

Four Essential Ingredients of Good Self-Care

While each of us is unique in what restores us, good self-care involves four essential ingredients: sleep, prayer, movement, and relationship. We need about eight to ten hours a day of self-care to be able to raise children and live in a marriage. Sound crazy? It's not only possible but also necessary.

Here is how good self-care breaks down. It starts with sleeping seven to nine hours every night. If we want to start better self-care habits, the one thing that will get us the most bang for our buck is getting a good night's rest every night. Many of us don't do that, and the effects can be damaging. A 2013 Gallup poll showed that, in the United States, 40 percent of adults get less sleep than they need.[1] When we don't sleep, we increase our risk of serious health problems such as obesity, heart problems (heart attacks, heart failure, irregular heartbeat), high blood pressure, stroke, and diabetes. We also increase the chances of irritability, inattentiveness, and lack of emotional presence.

Once we start getting a good seven to nine hours of sleep each night, then we can focus on the other two hours. We need thirty to forty-five minutes of reflection, meditation, and/or prayer in the morning before we start our day. The benefits of incorporating this into our routines are far better than being able to check the quiet-time box on our spiritual report cards. The relationship between prayer and health has been the subject of much scientific research. Dr. Herbert Benson at Harvard Medical School discovered what he calls "the relaxation response," which occurs during periods of prayer and meditation.[2] At such times, the body's metabolism decreases, the heart rate slows, blood pressure goes down, and breathing becomes calmer and more regular. This is vital because over half of all doctor visits in the United States today are prompted by illnesses connected to stress and anxiety, such as depression, high blood pressure, ulcers, migraine headaches, and a general lack of energy.[3]

The third thing we need is thirty to forty-five minutes a day of moving our bodies. Just like we need time to replenish our internal worlds, we need time to take care of our bodies. Doing so doesn't require joining a gym or hiring a personal trainer. Self-care can be as simple as a good walk in the morning or at lunch or after dinner as a family. Just moving will benefit us immensely. If you already work out, great. If you don't, start by walking thirty minutes a day. If that is all the movement you do for yourself, it will be more beneficial for you as a person and a parent than making promises and starting programs and diets you will likely quit.

The final thing we need to do with our remaining self-care time is build relationships with friends. Women need time with women. Men need time with men. Moms and dads both need authentic and vibrant relationships in which they share their hearts with people of the same sex outside the nuclear family. We need relationships in which our hearts are fed, but too often moms and dads end up feeling afraid, ashamed, and guilty for developing close friends.

Paradoxically, men teach men how to love women, and women teach women how to love men. Men need to spend time with other men, and women need to spend time with other women. When doing so, they need to take the risk of telling the truth about their lives. This involves more than just reporting the events of the day. They need to speak their hearts to one another. Too often the exhaustion we feel as parents (and spouses) is due to a lack of emotional and spiritual intimacy with friends.

When my (Chip's) sons were growing up, Sonya would get together with other women and say, "My house is so full of testosterone that I don't even have a voice over there." By the time the boys were in high school, Sonya had three guys all over six feet tall. Loud. Rough. Hungry. Smelly. I witnessed so many times when Sonya would spend time with other women and would come home replenished. She would go walking with a friend and come back and her mood would be lighter and she would no longer be consumed by all the things that needed to be done.

Now, if you are going out with your friends to run away from facing your life, that is different than going out with them so that you can tell the truth to each other about life. Time is precious. When the time we take for ourselves is spent goofing off and postponing reality, we are going to be more resentful and lonely and inevitably will want to spend more time getting away.

As stated above, men need to be with men to find replenishment. Women need to be with women to find replenishment. There is only so much a man can give a woman and a woman can give a man. Men have to be loved by other men to be able to love a woman. If men don't know how to be with men, they too often demand their wives make them a man—and women aren't good at helping men be men. It just doesn't work. When a man expects a woman to make him a man, he's setting that woman up to be a mother or a mistress. He will try to make her a sex object or a caretaker. He will look to her for relief, not relationship. And often a woman will settle for being either a sex object or a caretaker with her husband rather than a woman. This dynamic means that the marriage is draining and not replenishing—and children in this dynamic suffer.

The same is also true for women. Women need to be with other women to be able to love a man. When they don't spend time with other women, they try to share their lives (as a mom, wife, daughter, sister, friend, leader, etc.) with their husbands, and too often they are left feeling lonely and misunderstood. Their husbands become economic objects or coworkers.

The four elements of self-care will energize the emotional and spiritual intimacy in a marriage, and a vibrant marriage has a synergistic effect that benefits the children in the family even more.

Gettin' Needy

We all have an internal GPS that continually answers God's first question: "Where are you?" (Gen. 3:9). This is an intimate question that invites us to share our hearts. Answering that question honestly requires an emotional response. God is always checking in with us. And God desires us to check in with ourselves to report our needs.

To be full-hearted parents and to engage in regenerative self-care, we need to listen to the voices of our hearts and become aware of our feelings and needs so that we can attend to our true selves. As we do, we will learn more about ourselves and God. Much of self-care is the willingness to acknowledge our needs and to learn how to get those needs met.

Self-care is a posture of listening to ourselves and learning. To be good at self-care, we need to be adept at listening to our needs. Chip's book *Needs of the Heart* contains a thorough discussion of some of the basic emotional and spiritual human needs. Here is a brief summary.

Belonging: the need to be accepted for who we are as emotional and spiritual beings

Mattering: the need to be appreciated for our individual giftedness

Security: the need to have a "place" where we can struggle and be supported in the struggle

Touch: the need for physical (nonsexual) nurturing

Grief: the need to experience and express the cost of the losses we experience in daily life

Attention: the need to be recognized, tended to, cared for, and even nurtured

Sexuality: the need to feel and express comfort in our own skin as men and women

Guidance: the need for others to show us how to go where we have never been in life

Accomplishment: the need to (1) know when we have reached marginal diminishing returns and that it is time to stop; (2) celebrate the rewards of having given ourselves to something that matters to us; (3) rest as we move toward the completion of that which moves us

Support: the need for continual response to and replenishment of our ongoing needs

Listening and trust: the need for others to receive our hearts while we speak about the parts of our lives that matter most to us; the need for the one who is listening to be there for us

Freedom: the need to be free from tyranny that stops us from living fully, loving deeply, and leading well

Fun/play: the need to engage in activities in which we can be fully human and not be self-conscious or self-critical

Identifying these needs allows us to know what kind of care we need to craft for ourselves. Admission of our neediness leads us to be responsible, intentional, and wise.

Impaired Attempts at Self-Care

When self-care is not approached from an internal awareness of the true self, we too often turn to impaired—though effective—ways of caring for ourselves. Mood altering and multitasking are two of the most common forms of impaired attempts at self-care that parents use.

Mood altering is one version of impaired self-care. Many of us are familiar and have been personally affected by the three major mood alterers: alcohol, drugs (prescription and illicit), and sex/lust. We humans are infinitely creative in developing impaired relationships with mood-altering substances, behaviors, and/or processes. These include:

- anxiety/control
- work
- sleep
- rage
- gambling
- eating (or not eating)
- exercise
- television
- electronics (social media, games, email, texting)
- video games
- televised sports
- children's activities
- religion
- practiced depression (not to be confused with neurologically based depressive disorders)
- entertainment (movies and music)

Another version of impaired self-care comes in the form of multitasking. No matter how hard we try, humans are not capable of emotional multitasking. We are created to relate to one thing at a time. Our attempts to multitask lead us to a lack of emotional and spiritual presence—which ultimately results in our not being able to love well. True emotional and spiritual freedom can be found only when we break the cycle of thinking we can control outcomes and let the proverbial balls we are juggling fall to the ground. The freedom of surrendering control is profound.

Excuses and Misunderstandings

When we bring up the issue of self-care at conferences—especially if the audience has Christians in it—we get questions such as "If I'm a Christian, am I not supposed to take up my cross and put others first? Doesn't loving others mean I put myself last?"

To answer simply, no. We don't agree with that. We are made to receive from God so we can give to others. We need to be good at receiving care that allows us to give from abundance, not scarcity. When we habitually martyr ourselves in relationship, we put ourselves in the place of God. "Taking up your cross" means to carry the burden of love. We are made to pick up the pain of life every day, walk in it, and love others really well. We are made to live in a story filled with hope and not avoid the hard things—the seemingly impossible things—that come in our lives. We are made to practice living in such a way that we trust that God is doing something good—something more than we can even ask or imagine. As parents, we are called to carry the heartache of our children, and if we do—as Jesus did—it will break our own hearts. All those things are the cross we bear.

The only way we are going to be able to live in that level of pain and service is if we do not think of ourselves as Jesus. Rather, as people of faith, we need to let Christ's active work do for us that which we could never do for ourselves. We live in the mercy we have received and become merciful to ourselves. The mercy we receive begins in our neediness.

When Jesus was asked what was most important, he said, "'Love the Lord your God with all your heart and with all your soul and with all your strength and with all your mind'; and, 'Love your neighbor as yourself.' . . . Do this and you will live" (Luke 10:27–28).

The "love your neighbor as yourself" part of the equation involves self-care. Another way of saying this is "We love others (even our kids) as we love ourselves." If we only serve, give, and sacrifice and never receive, we will be empty (and increasingly bitter). Self-care is about making sure we give out of our fullness and abundance and not our depletion and scarcity. We let our cups run over with goodness and mercy, and those around us get the overflow.

For many Christians, "lay down your life, take up your cross, and follow me" almost always gets interpreted as "do more." But we need to think about what this idea really means.

Laying down our lives and picking up our cross daily has more to do with putting down our agendas (self-will) and letting go of our egos (false self) so that we are available to practice trusting the rhythm of the kingdom, to go where we are called with what we have to offer. Most of the time sacrificing ourselves doesn't make things much better. When we are open and still and present, we can better recognize what we have to offer to those in need around us. Participating and showing up in the lives of our children in this way blesses them.

When we begin to lay down our egos and surrender our agendas, we become increasingly more available to what God is inviting us to participate in. This is different from working hard to make the world a good place. It's a different posture. It's a more loving, gentle, gracious, and generous posture (a much more Jesus-type approach). The self-willed agenda is an agenda that says, "Do your best. Do better. Do more." We become human doings instead of human beings.

Using People for Self-Care

It took me (Stephen) several years into marriage and parenthood to begin to understand how essential self-care is for me to be the husband, father, friend, and person I desire to be. For many years, I did not take care of myself in any legitimate, sustainable way. I rarely took time to restore, re-energize, and recover. I had this idea that if I were to "focus on myself," something bad would happen at home. I was deeply codependent. I carried a belief that it was my job to make sure others were happy. The closer I was to someone, the more responsible I felt for their feelings and needs. In short, I wasn't okay if they weren't okay. This was nowhere more true than in my relationship with Heather and her relationship with our kids.

I lived with an illusion that I was being *selfless* when actually I was entirely self-focused. I had little of my true self to give to others. My self-care was rooted in self-preservation—well-honed emotional survival strategies held over from my childhood. I could not articulate this at the time, but because of the wounds I had experienced and the vows I had made against how God had created me, I believed, "If I can make

145

others okay, then I can stay in control, and they will need me. I will never be alone, and most importantly, I will not be hurt." I thought I knew better than God.

I lacked the emotional maturity and spiritual wisdom to recognize my needs, reasonably care for myself, and responsibly care for others. There was no way I was going to risk hanging out with some close guy friends one night a week, exercising in the evening a couple times a week, or, God forbid, taking a weekend trip with some buddies two to three times a year. In the name of being loving, I was being selfish. My core, toxic, shame-based beliefs kept me from letting people truly know and love me for me. At that time in my life, I believed that my value came from what I could do for others or what success I could achieve. I did not believe that God delighted in and enjoyed me. Whether I could recognize it or not, I lived as if God required me to be good and do better. I could not fathom that God was not in perpetual disappointment with me. This way of living led to all kinds of secret resentments toward Heather, the kids, myself, and God.

Like many people, I lived on an island in the middle of an emotional Bermuda Triangle of anxiety/depression, shame, and self-reliance. In my heart, questions circled like hungry sharks just below the waterline: What do I do next? What if the other shoe drops? What if someone really sees the true me? I became a codependent mess. I needed Heather and our kids to be okay so I could be okay with myself.

Codependency is the reliance on others' approval for our own well-being. (I am okay only if you are okay with me.) The more we love someone and want to receive love from that person, the more at risk of codependency we are. While many adults struggle with similar patterns of relationship with themselves, others, and God, this self-centered preoccupation is often most acute between parents and children (and husbands and wives). In relationships between parents and children, this codependent energy can flow one of three ways.

One way is parent to child. In this pattern of relationship, the parent lacks the ability to tolerate the child's disappointment and disgust. In this scenario, the parent can become excessively reliant on the child's happiness for their own sense of peace, and the parent orders their world around the emotional life of the child. "If little Johnny/Jill is not happy, then Mom and/or Dad is not happy." This shows up in all kinds of situations throughout the lifetime of the relationship between the parent and the child—from nap time to preschool to the ball field to college to a wedding to taking care of grandchildren—but it is primarily marked by the parent's inability to tell the child no.

In the second codependent parenting style, the child is overly responsible for the parent's sense of security. Two things happen in this dynamic. The first is that the child sees it as their job to make sure Dad and Mom are taken care of and don't get too upset or frustrated. The second is that the parent lets the child emotionally comfort them, encourage them, and overcompensate for something the parent lacks. In this relationship, the parent expects an unhealthy level of devotion, love, appreciation, and respect from the child. Too often the parent is trying to get the child to make up for what they lack in other relationships—often trying to get from the child the affirmation and/or attention they wished they would have gotten from their own parents. Parents who have not yet taken responsibility for their own emotional and spiritual needs, lack healthy intimacy in their marriages and other adult relationships, and carry unhealed toxic shame often look to their children to satiate their wounded hearts.

The third kind of impaired relationship between parent and child is a combination of the previous two: parent to child to parent. In this style, the parent and the child have a deeply enmeshed relationship with each other marked by a significant lack of healthy boundaries. At best, this relationship is marked by anxiety, and at worst, it is akin to emotional incest. The relationship is knotted, and neither the parent nor the child is free to be themselves. A close parent-child relationship is not in and of itself a problem, but when the boundaries of the relationship become blurred, it leads to confusion regarding the roles and responsibilities of both the parent and the child. This relational confusion is devastating to both and will have profound effects on the child as they move into adulthood, marriage, and their own parenting. Untangling this enmeshment is hard and important work.

These three impaired relationship styles can vary in degree of severity. A parent can be more or less codependent with their child depending on how they are doing in their own life. In addition, each type of codependency between parent and child is often different with different children within the same family. A dad or mom may relate to their son in the first style (parent to child) and their daughter in the third style (parent to child to parent) and their third child in the second style (child to parent). In intergenerational families (more than two generations living together), blended families (a family consisting of a couple and their children from the current and all previous relationships), or both together, relationships can become a codependent mosh pit of relational dysfunction. But fundamentally, all three of these patterns of relationship lead to the same place. They reduce the child's ability to develop emotional resiliency, maintain relational intimacy, possess spiritual vitality, and forge and maintain their own identity. The child's sense of self is traded in favor of the relational needs of the parent.

One way you can tell the level of codependency you carry is by asking yourself these questions. In your life now (or when you were growing up), do you (or did you):

- believe you cause other people's feelings
- believe you can put someone in a bad mood or a good mood
- believe you can make someone do something with your actions
- believe you can read minds (you know what people need without them saying it)
- watch others to see what to do to make them okay so you would be okay

If we were raised in a family of codependency and have not addressed our issues sufficiently, we will more than likely raise our children the same way. Perhaps we were raised to get our identity from pleasing our parents. When we grow up and have our own children, we think that being responsible for them means anticipating their needs, fixing their feelings, and reading their minds, and we think that doing these things equals love—but it actually equals control. It is our attempt to try to keep our children from feeling, from needing, from expressing, even from making mistakes they need to make in order to learn. We try to maintain control so that we don't wind up feeling as if we are going to get in trouble ourselves.

If we come from an environment like that, it's almost inevitable that we have a difficult time taking care of ourselves and that the idea of something happening to our children that causes them sadness or hurt or fear means we somehow have to fix it or we have failed as a parent. Failing our children really means we might wind up not having love anymore, because if we shape our identity around the pleasure of another person, we are living in the fear that if they don't have pleasure, the love will end.

Refilling

Anything that is empty needs to be refilled. So our job is to continuously let ourselves be refilled, because a child's security is in the strength of the parent. And the strength of the parent is their capacity to let themselves be replenished so they can stay strong. We stay strong only through the irony of neediness. Being needy is one of the great gifts we can give to our children because our neediness continues to make our hearts strong to participate with them.

Jesus spent a great deal of time resting. The larger the crowds, the more Jesus would go off alone and pray and find refreshment. Jesus took many naps and rested and played and ate with friends and shared and received a lot. His life was shaped around and his heart was fed by an intimate community of close friends. (Peter, James, John, Mary, Martha, and Lazarus were some of his closest companions in the Scriptures.) Jesus was good at being responsible with his neediness.

I (Chip) got up one morning when I was in Israel and ran the six miles from Jerusalem to Bethlehem at 5:30 as the day was breaking. I caught a bus back to Jerusalem after buying two watermelons to share with my friends. While I was running, I thought about how long it would take to walk from Jerusalem to Bethlehem. Jesus and the disciples walked the six miles and took their time doing so. I pictured them talking and learning from Jesus, even sitting in the shade under trees on the way. They talked, prayed, even laughed. From a "time is money" perspective, Jesus wasted a lot of time. He spent time praying, resting, eating, and laughing when he could have been preaching and healing. Think about that. He spent a lot of time restoring himself and talking to his Father, then talking and sharing with his friends, instead of healing and teaching people.

The greatest fruits come out of the deepest roots, and roots require a lot of feeding to produce. So the more well fed we are, the more we can create. Growth, maturity, and wisdom are more about receiving than producing. We can't give what we do not have. If, as parents, we want our children to be secure, confident, wise, and present, then we better have those things in our own lives so we can give them to our children.

GOING DEEPER

- Are you able to tolerate your children's disappointments and discouragements, or do you try to fix them/solve them?

- How free are your children not to try to take care of your feelings or flee from your feelings?
- What is something you really enjoy that you have not pursued in a long time? What would it take for you to begin to reengage that activity?
- What do you need to stop doing today? To what do you need to say no?

SEVEN

Climb the Mountain of Their Dreams

The glory of God is man fully alive, and
the life of man is the vision of God.

Saint Irenaeus

Once we grasp the importance and behaviors of self-care, then we are more prepared to step into the full responsibility of helping our children fully live the distinctive stories that are being written into their lives. Each child is created as a unique image bearer of God. They are created to see who they are made to be and do what they are made to do, to live a story that reveals the character of who created them. No two people reflect or reveal God's glory the same way. We as parents are called to deeply engage our children in order to help them discover and live fully into who they are created to become. Our ultimate responsibility as parents is to do whatever is possible to help our children live their unique stories to the fullest. We call this opportunity helping them climb the mountain of their dreams.

From the moment we learn we are becoming parents, we carry dreams and ideas of who we wish our children will become. We anticipate and wonder about the details of their lives. We pledge not to let them repeat our mistakes. We pray for rich blessing in their lives. We imagine who they will be, and we hope for what their lives can be.

Again and again throughout our lives with our children, our hearts will come into conflict with the dreams and wishes for our children that do not fit the reality of what is occurring in our children's lives. Our hopes, imaginings, prayers, pledges, anticipations, ideas, and dreams will never squarely line up with who our children are created to be and the stories they are to inhabit. The way our children are created and their proclivities, gifts, interests, curiosities, and callings often do not create the exact stories that we dream for them. Their stories might be a version of our dreams, but they never have the exact same scripts. They may not have the exact grades, the exact friend group, the exact haircut, the exact height, the exact weight, the exact spouse, the exact outcomes. It is guaranteed that their stories will be different from what we hoped they would be. At times, their lives will be far more wonderful than we could have ever dreamed, asked, or imagined for them. Other times we will wonder if there is any obvious rhyme or reason to the stories they are living. And there will be times, too, when we will be confused and crushed by life's twisted tragedies that abruptly break their hearts and ours with them.

If we are honest with ourselves, we must let go of the stories we want to write for our children and come to embrace the stories that God is writing for them. Some parents face this right from the beginning. We'd hoped for a boy and got a girl. Maybe we planned to get pregnant and instead were led down the road of adoption. Or maybe we were surprised to learn that our child had a significant health issue or genetic disorder. Other times the discrepancies between our dreams and their stories subtly reveal themselves over many years. We must carry in our hearts the admonition of Solomon that can be paraphrased as "raise up a child in the way the child is created, and when the child is of age, the child will not depart from who they are created to become" (see Prov. 22:6).

Tools for the Climb

There are things our children need from us emotionally and spiritually if they are going to climb the mountain of their dreams. Our main assignment as parents is to advance them into having a life beyond us. The proverb says, "Train up a child in the way he should go; even when he is old he will not depart from it" (Prov. 22:6 ESV). One way of understanding this proverb is that we should raise up a child based on the bent of the child, and when the child is older, able to leave us, and values and recognizes their own unique makeup, then they will not depart from trusting how they are created. Too often this proverb is turned into an instruction of imposing and molding and shaping and fitting a child into a form the parent has made—as if the child is born as a blank slate upon which the parent writes their own story for the child. The proverb is actually saying that each child is unique and has their own story, gifts, personality, interests, and way of being—which came with them at birth.

God has written a sentence upon our hearts that is unique to each person. Learning the full meaning of this sentence will take a lifetime, but our job as parents is to pay attention to our children, to listen to their hearts, and to begin to help nurture and name their unique stories. We and our children are made to participate in creating beauty—each of us in our own unique way.

While climbing the mountain of their dreams requires action and investment, the journey is also an inward journey they take through the territory of their own hearts. Because of this, to help our children climb the mountain of their dreams, we must engage them on a heart level in the following key ways:

- read them
- name them
- draw them out
- encourage them
- release them

Read Them

We have to be very good readers of our children's stories. Reading the stories written on their hearts requires that we are close enough to know our children's wounds, shame, and limitations as well as their "God-madeness," dignity, and passions. This means parenting with a posture of curiosity and appreciation about who they are and what God is doing in their lives. Along with David Thomas, I (Stephen) touched on this in our book *Wild Things: The Art of Nurturing Boys*.

We don't need to keep a scientific log on our [children], but we do need to pay attention to the mundane details of their lives. We need to listen well to what is said and not said. We need to linger with them long enough to study them and to hear from them (even if they aren't saying much). We need to listen to what they are saying about themselves when they tell stories—and discern what they are not saying as well. We need to watch them when they interact with their peers and gather feedback from other adults who care for them.[1]

Name Them

When we "see" our children as separate from our own creation, we can then speak into who we have come to know. As parents, we have a spiritual responsibility and authority in our children's lives to declare the truth about them, to them, and for them. This is what it means to name the hearts of our children. On an emotional and spiritual level, naming our children has nothing to do with what is on their birth certificates. Putting into words what we have come to know about the truth of our children's hearts can be a tremendous blessing because when we do so, we point them toward their identity, promise, and God-madeness. When we speak to the truth of our children—with accuracy and wisdom—our words will be the trusted guideposts our children can depend on for their entire lives.

The converse is equally true. When not used constructively in love, naming can send children off course, and it may take decades for them to recover. While sticks and stones may break our bones, it's often the words that scar our hearts. We possess great power to cut the hearts of our children with daggers of insult, dismissal, and diminishment. When we misuse the authority of naming our children, the invisible wounds of shame can be carried for a long time. Words can have a very long shelf life.

Draw Them Out

For our children to climb the mountain of their dreams, we need to encourage, challenge, invite, woo, and direct their hearts toward expressing passion, living in intimacy, and walking in integrity. Our children need our help in knowing how and when to express what is stirring within them. Even with loving and engaged parents present in their lives, children learn from an early age to hide their hearts and disguise who they really are. Much of parenting the heart of a child is like playing hide-and-seek. In regard to our children's hearts, we need to ask ourselves, "Where are they today? Where did they go?"

As much as we want to believe the best in our children, we also have to face that they can be deceitful and sneaky. What they tell us is not always true. Sometimes even when they are trying to be honest, they lack the insight and life experiences to make themselves known well. Even if storming the hearts of our children like a SWAT team could be done, doing so would be ill-advised. A far subtler approach is needed to help our children express their hearts. Our children can't figure out their lives on their own. Similar to the way a horse whisperer works with horses, we can help draw out our children and guide them toward who they are made to be. This process has far more to do with intimacy than instruction, with building relationship than mastering content. Intimacy is about "into-me-see" or experiencing another person. Instruction is about performing, doing, and mastering. To *be* in relationship is vastly different from teaching our children *about* life. To draw them out, we need to ask our children questions such as:

- What do you need?
- What are you feeling?
- What are your dreams?
- What was that like for you?
- What do you think?

Encourage Them

Because coming down is always easier than climbing up, our children will need a lot of encouragement if they are going to climb the mountain of their dreams. The etymology of the word *encouragement* is interesting. The word comes from the early fifteenth-century Old French word *encoragier*, which means "to make strong, hearten." When we break it down, the word literally means "to put in" (en-) "heart" (courage).

There will be times when our children are going to be tempted to lose heart, and they will struggle with questions such as "Do I have what it takes?" and "Am I worth it?" When these times come, our children need us to help them keep heart. They need to be genuinely cheered on, empathized with, supported, and affirmed in the struggle but not over-promised, placated, or falsely reassured. As parents, we need to pay attention to where our children are headed. We are called to bring everything we have to their lives. The more heart we have, the more we have to bring. The more passion, intimacy, and integrity we have in our own lives, the more we can genuinely show up in their lives.

Release Them

The final practice may be the most difficult part of helping them climb the mountain of their dreams. In order for our children to climb the mountain of their dreams, we as parents have to be really good at turning our children over to the will of God—and the God we have writes far more painful, joyous, and "surpassing" stories in our children's lives than we would ever be able to write for them. If we were writing their stories, all our children would get the gold medal. Sure, we'd probably put in just enough struggle for them to think they earned it, but in the end, they would be happy, wealthy, and wise with ease.

God doesn't seem afraid to let heartache, pain, and brokenness into our lives. Those are some of the primary elements God uses to shape our hearts and our lives so that we become instruments of love and instruments of God's bigger story—and that is a scary proposition as the parent of a child.

Safe, Flat Lands

Very often we will try to keep our children from climbing the mountain of their dreams so that they don't have to deal with heartache and/or so that we don't have to deal with heartache. But when we do this controlling behavior, we are forcing our children to be less than they are made to be.

Our efforts to keep them on the flat ground of low expectations will keep them safe but will also keep them from God. They will never have to be challenged with life's tough questions, such as where God went or if God even really cares. Their god will be small and manageable and explainable—none of which God is—because they will never really be in a place where their hearts are at risk of being broken.

If they climb, there is a guarantee they will slip. They will fall. They will get hurt. They will most likely fail because longings are greater within us than reality will allow. They will have to experience some form of deprivation. They will have to ask the hard questions of themselves, of us, and of God.

I (Chip) remember a time when our two sons were in pretty big, separate worlds but similar crises of the heart. Sonya said to me, "I think we messed up how we raised them."

"Well, definitely, that's for sure. There's no doubt about that," I said.

She continued, "We raised them with so much hope. They're getting so hurt by life. What if it's wrong that we raised them to dare to believe that they can live life through the eyes of their hearts?" Like many of us, Sonya grew up practicing the belief "If you don't get your hopes up, you won't be disappointed and you won't get hurt."

I answered, "No, no, no. I'm scared too, but no. They are made to live with heart, and sometimes that means they are going to get hurt. I wish otherwise, but let's just hang on to hope." We raised our sons to hope, to dream, to be hurt, and to dream again. We gave them room to grieve. We gave them room to celebrate. Living in this way hurts more because it's worth more. Of course, we messed up like crazy and tried to control them too. But this truth I knew: for better or worse, we are created to hope and hope greatly come what may.

We and our children are made to experience the fullness of life, to live the entire scale from one to ten. Too often, though, we begin to see how high the mountains are and end up creating for ourselves (by trying to manufacture for our children) a predictable and tame world in which we can all live between five and five. But a world between five and five doesn't exist. We as parents need to admit to ourselves that a part of us doesn't want our children to have a full life. We want them to have a safe and happy life. If we can't tolerate our children climbing anything higher than anthills, we will make sure that their dreams are small and manageable or, worse, given up on completely.

The Wrong Mountains

Another mistake we as parents make in this area is that we send our children to climb the wrong mountains. When we burden our children with our egos and heartaches, we make our children prisoners of our past. This happens in two ways. Either we prod them to pursue the same things we achieved and in which we found security, or we marshal them into pursuing the lost causes of our failures and unrealized dreams.

Children are not made to climb the mountains of their parents' dreams. Children cannot find their true identity in propping up the egos of their parents. Children cannot discover who they are made to be in God by cleaning up their parents' pasts. They are not made to become the all-star, valedictorian, beauty queen, or rock star just because their parents did or didn't.

Christian parents talk a lot about wanting their children to have a heart for God. But who really wants their child to be like David—a man after God's own heart? Sure, he was brave, confident in God, a good friend, a poet, and a leader. He always eventually sought forgiveness deeply and genuinely. But he was also a forgotten son, an adulterer, a liar, and a murderer. When he was sad, he grieved fully (ripping his clothes, not eating, crying, throwing dirt on his head), and when he was grateful, he threw big parties (dancing in his undergarments and playing loud music). He was wild at heart. We are tempted to read the Bible and make David a hero-king figure. For sure, that is part of the story. But the part that makes it believable and God amazing is the human struggle that is the rest of the story.

We too often don't consider what it means to raise a child to be a person after God's own heart. Most commonly, what we are really talking about when we talk about parenting is how to raise a Goliath while talking a lot about David. We want our children to be successful, tough, standouts, respected, even feared—we want winners. We want our children to become impenetrable people who won't be taken down by life, who are giants, who are attractive, and who are strong instead of people who feel everything, as David expressed so eloquently throughout the Psalms.

If you have stopped climbing the mountain of your own dreams or have saddled your children with your past, the best you can hope for is that your children will break relationship with you and take their hearts to others who can handle their groans. That way they can pursue who God made them to become instead of who you have tried to mold them into.

Make sure that as a parent you are climbing the mountain of your own dreams. We can only help our children live into their stories to the degree that we have lived into our own. This is worth repeating again: we can't give our children what we do not have. If we can't tolerate the pain of climbing the mountain of our own imagination, desires, and longings; if we can't tolerate failure, hurt, loss, and disappointment; if we can't receive hope and celebration; if we don't know the fear associated with stepping into the unknown to discover faith, then we can't be with our children as far as they need us. Our gift to our children is our own human experience.

God's Territory

When we release our children and bless them to climb the mountain of their dreams, we have become willing to let them have their hearts broken and their hearts filled. Our responsibility as good-enough parents is to send our children on a quest for a full life, knowing that the higher they climb up the mountain of their dreams, the farther they have to fall. We dream for them. We dream with them. Life will never turn out exactly like we wished it would, however. It will turn out like it does instead.

So much of maturing in life and in faith is learning to trust the story of God, which is wild and unpredictable and uncaged and far more beautiful than the organized and produced lives we try to create for ourselves. Many of us work really hard to have a life that is just as predictable as other people's lives appear to be. That life dares little and risks even less. It ends up being a life focused on the approval of others. It's not a life novels are written about. It's not the substance of Scripture. Anyone of note in Scripture experienced some kind of great heartache. The people who were the closest to God often had the most difficult struggles: betrayal, failure, devastation. But they also had extraordinary celebration. It's so wonderful to say, "I'm going to help my child climb the mountain of their dreams." However, we must recognize that in doing so, we are also signing up for a mountain of struggle, heartbreak, and sorrow. Being a good-enough parent means we are willing to walk with them through it all—the sorrows and the joys—because life's experiences are all tied together.

GOING DEEPER

- Reflect on areas of your life in which you have stopped having your own dreams for yourself. Begin to explore again the aspects of naming yourself, drawing yourself out, and encouraging yourself to do something real, something purposeful for your heart/passions/desires. Journal or write a letter to yourself or to God about those hopes and the fears that go along with them. Maybe sign up for a class, join a team, start a book club—whatever it is that brings you joy.
- Practice letting your children leave the house with dirty faces. In messy clothes. Embrace letting your children be themselves and not fretting over what others will think of your parenting.

- Talk to your spouse or a friend about the ways your fear leads you to parent in the "safe lands" or to encourage your kids to climb the "wrong mountains." This is another chance to explore your unfinished business and get feedback from those you trust.

EIGHT

Hold the Flag Brave and True

Give me liberty or give me death.

Patrick Henry

"Raising the Flag on Iwo Jima," a photograph by Associated Press photographer Joe Rosenthal, was arguably one of the most significant photographs of the twentieth century. Taken on February 23, 1945, it depicts six United States Marines raising an American flag atop Mount Suribachi during the Battle of Iwo Jima in World War II. It became a symbol of the Pacific theater and an icon of American culture, and it speaks to more than the moment it captured. This image became the basis for a sculpture called the United States Marine Corps War Memorial, which is dedicated to every marine who has died in combat since November 10, 1775.

An inscription that appears inside a victor's wreath on the granite base borrows words spoken by Fleet Admiral

Chester W. Nimitz to the sailors and marines who fought at Iwo Jima. It reads, "Uncommon valor was a common virtue." The marine motto *Semper Fidelis*—"always faithful"—is inscribed on the ribbon underneath the wreath.

The historic moment from 1945 was the united effort of six men to raise an American flag on the summit. The photo re-creates the scene with a larger fifty-six-inch by ninety-six-inch flag so everyone could clearly see that the Americans had reached the summit. The event marked the turning point of a bloody thirty-six-day battle to gain control of the small island.

Throughout history, flags have been important symbols. In past times, when armies would go to battle, the regiments and units within the armies would have flag bearers. The soldier who held the flag was responsible for carrying the distinctive mark of the unit or regiment. The flag bearer gave everyone a visual reference as to where the unit or regiment was as chaos inevitably ensued. When soldiers would get separated from their units, they would look for the standard-bearer so they would know what to do.

Standard-bearers were often killed because carrying the flag made them a target of the other army for two reasons. First, taking the flag was strategic. Without a raised standard, the unit members did not have a visual point to push toward, return to, or organize around. Second, losing a flag in battle was one of the worst things that could happen. It was akin to losing the collective honor of the unit. From the armies of the Roman Empire to the armies of the US Civil War, the "colors" represented honor and dignity. Therefore, when a flag bearer went down, it was the duty and honor of the other members of the company to pick up the standard and carry it. The loss of the colors was a tragic loss, indicating that the unit, regiment, or army had been defeated.

Our children are made to grow into people who can separate from us. They are made to leave us and step into their own quest to live fully, love deeply, and lead well as they climb the mountain of their dreams. They keep heart in this lofty endeavor by holding tightly to and flying high the standards and values that can help them stay truehearted in their quest. As we help them climb the mountain of their dreams, we must also help them hold the flag brave and true—to keep the voice of the heart alive.

Resources for Flag Bearers

As children grow, they are faced with many decisions that will shape their lives. These moments of truth are seminal ingredients that make up who they are becoming. Children follow a long and winding road to becoming grown-ups. As they work through the stages of childhood, they are hopefully learning to navigate a life that sometimes feels more like a maze than a path. Their ability to abide in the common values and principles that have been encouraged in them by their parents and communities is vital to helping them negotiate the needed and inevitable internal struggles, relational conflicts, and moral challenges they will face. Their ability to hold the flag brave and true becomes one of the primary resources they have in this process and has at least four components: recognizing a big story, keeping things simple, growing the voices of their hearts, and realizing that behavior is not the goal.

Recognizing a Big Story

One of the essential elements of holding the flag brave and true is recognizing that the flag represents being part of something bigger than oneself. Our children live out their unique stories within the bigger story of God. They need to know they are a part of God's story, one that is continuing to be written. Their passions, purposes, and plans are a reflection of the image of God they bear. Their hearts' assignment is to participate fully in knowing how they are created, to live fully, and to do what they are made to do—make a difference.

They are gifted, and they live in a world in need. Where there is darkness, they can bring light. Where there is despair, they can bring hope. Where there is destruction, they can bring creativity and construction. Where there is loss and death, they can bring courage. This is full-hearted participation in doing what they are called to do.

We are all created to focus on and participate in "whatever is true, whatever is noble, whatever is right, whatever is pure, whatever is lovely, whatever is admirable . . . excellent or praiseworthy" (Phil. 4:8). In other words, we participate in the bigger story; we are a part of it. We don't write the story; we serve as noble characters in the story. Note the word *serve*. We are made to find our place in the bigger story as we grow into being of maximum service. We are not responsible for the outcome; we are responsible for participating.

The bigger the story our children are connected to, the better off they will be. There is safety in knowing that we are part of a bigger story. It relieves the pressure, shame, and loneliness that a person can experience if their story is small and self-serving. Small can ironically mean that everything is about them, that the universe exists to serve them. When a child carries a story that is just about them or their family, they can feel as if they are the center of the universe—whether it's their own universe or their parents'. This kind of pressure and self-serving attitude stunts the growth and maturity of the child's heart. Their outside grows, but inside they live under a tyranny of shame because they have been assigned the task of shaping the universe.

Keeping It Simple

Another key component of holding the flag brave and true is not making things overly complex. When life gets challenging, if our children have to navigate a complex scheme or code of right/wrong, good/bad rules, they end up grounding their lives in performance. When they are put in positions of emotional stress, they will focus on external approval more than on internal motivation and values. Courage to stand up for one's own convictions is a matter of the heart. If children only know how to follow the rules, they are under the control of peer pressure. As they grow, they are more concerned about doing something right than about being true to who they are made to be. Performance-driven families turn love into something to be earned, and security is always temporary. Self-worth is only as good as one's last performance. If a family or a culture has a lot of shoulds and should nots, the children will be fear- and shame-based in their thinking. Shoulds will rule their lives.

Many of the Pharisees in Scripture added rule upon rule to try to do the right thing and make themselves worthy before

God. This was one of the groups Jesus had the hardest time with and the harshest words for. When asked by a teacher of the law which of all the commandments were the most important, Jesus boiled down all the law and all the commandments to two things: "'Love the Lord your God with all your heart and with all your soul and with all your mind and with all your strength.' The second is this: 'Love your neighbor as yourself.' There is no commandment greater than these" (Mark 12:30–31). That's pretty clear. That's keeping it simple.

The simple standard that Jesus offered turns us away from the law and inward to self-examination and relationship with God and others. What does it mean to love? How do we love ourselves? How do we love our neighbor? What does it mean to love the one true God? The metaphor that Jesus is pointing to is that the law is a scroll, but the scroll is useless unless it hangs from two pegs so that it can be unrolled and read and discussed and lived. All the laws, all the scrolls, hang from those two pegs, and without those pegs, there is no way to read the law and engage the scrolls. The ability to live the law requires internal motivation. Rules are fulfilled because we value relationship. "Doing unto others as I would have them do unto me" involves an internal awareness that my own heart is a doorway to another's. If children are focused on the approval of another, they cannot pay attention to their own hearts. They will lack empathy and awareness of how others may feel or think.

If our children have an internal awareness, they will not lose heart while they are trying to climb the mountain of their dreams. They will have values, a standard to bear as they face persecution, difficulty, struggle, and even success. They will be oriented in love of God, others, and themselves.

Growing the Voices of Their Hearts

To live into the bigger story and to maintain their internal standards, children will need to be supported in growing the voices of their hearts. They need to be good at knowing and articulating the emotional experiences of living: sadness, hurt, loneliness, fear, anger, gladness, shame, and guilt. Unless children are helped to know how to handle their feelings, they will avoid them or react against them—both of which are forms of denying the struggles of the heart. We all need to be good at feeling the feelings we are created to feel, because all of those feelings are gifts—gifts that allow us to live fully in a tragic place. Love that can tolerate only happiness is very thin. Robust love is expressed and true character is revealed during the painful and wonderful things that clearly expose the heart.

When children have a voice, they get to ask questions. I (Stephen) remember overhearing a conversation between a father and son in an airport restroom. In the time it took me to wash my hands, this boy asked a litany of questions to his father. "Daddy, why are there men in the stalls? Daddy, why are you washing your face? Daddy, why are the lights so bright? Daddy, why . . ." The son was machine-gunning his father with whatever questions were in his brain. As this was happening, two guys in the stalls couldn't help but start laughing, to which the boy asked, "Daddy, why are those men in the bathroom laughing?" His dad was an awesome dad because for every question, he said, "Well, son," and then he did his best to explain the lights and why he was washing his face and why those men were laughing in the bathroom. It was beautiful. He didn't say, "You're asking too many questions. I don't have time. Stop being silly."

Those four-year-old questions grow into more complex questions as children get older: "What happens when you die?" "Where do babies come from?" "Why is that person so sad?" If we can answer those questions honestly in age-appropriate ways, the questions will keep coming and will become even more complex as they grow: "Why are those kids mean to me at school?" "Why can't I sing like other kids?" "Why didn't I get invited?" They will come in and read Mom's or Dad's face and say, "What are you fighting about?" When tragedy hits, they can ask, "Where is God?" "Does God care?" "Is God good?" "Why did Granddad have to die?" "When will Daddy be back from rehab?" "Is it my fault that Mommy is so sad all the time?" As they get even older, questions emerge such as "Will I ever get married and have kids?" "Will I always be alone?" "Will I ever recover from the divorce?" "How will I face this diagnosis?"

Life's big questions don't have easy answers. The more children grow in heart, the harder it is to answer their questions. There aren't satisfying answers to the heart's deep questions. There aren't theological or psychological answers that will satisfy a broken heart. There is not a pat answer like, "Well, I've been to divinity school, gotten a PhD in psychology, am triple board-certified in medicine, and have an MBA, so let me tell you God's plan. It's going to be okay." Even if the answers are true conceptually, the heart's need for relationship means that we need someone to help us with the feelings more than the concepts we usually already grasp.

Our children need the voices of their internal worlds and our presence in their lives to help them keep heart so that they can, in turn, continue to live from the inside out. If they live controlled by the approval of others, they will lose the heart that God created them to have. They will lose the courage to be standard-bearers of a great story. People are most connected when they find acceptance in the struggles of their hearts. Without the voice of the heart revealed and accepted, concepts become empty answers.

Their ability to have confidence in their own thoughts, feelings, and needs will fortify them when the challenges come and they have to face the question "Which side are you on?" They will be able to answer, "This is where I stand. This is what I say. This is what I feel. This is what I need. This is what I want. This is what I hunger for. This is what I imagine. This is what I'm going to do. This is what is true, noble, right, pure, lovely, admirable, excellent, and praiseworthy."

Along with these questions, children are wondering about who they are. Our children need help in developing the ability to keep the voices of their hearts, even with us as parents, so that when the tough times come with others in their lives, they know what to do. Our children need to know how to tell the truth about who they are, what they feel and need, and what they think so that they can grow into people who can do the same with their spouses, their friends, and their own children later on.

The more we as parents can tolerate our own feelings and are supported in our lives by other adults, the more we can tolerate our children developing their own identity. We need to raise our children with the passion to have their own voices—not to be disrespectful but to speak up for who they are and what they need. If they can do that, they can live with passion—and a willingness to live in pain—for something that matters more than comfort. Without anger, they can't have passion. As parents, we need to have the courage to help our children hold on to and compassionately express their anger because only angry children will have a desire for life. Most people have a different concept of anger than what we are referring to here. Because anger is such a raw emotion it is often confused with rage and destruction. But true, pure anger is a creative force. (Other words for anger are yearning, desiring, hungering, thirsting, hoping, and wanting.) But our children need our help in knowing how to grow into their anger and direct it with wisdom. Here is an example.

My (Chip's) son William had great dreams of playing his sophomore year of high school baseball with Tennyson, who was in his senior year. Because of their age gap, they had never gotten to be on the field with each other before. This would be the year. They worked out together the summer and fall before the season, and William was on the starting team with his brother when the season started. In the second game, William got injured. The injury persisted for several weeks, sidelining him from his heart's dream after so many years.

One night after the injury, William and I were coming home from his youth group at church, and he was unusually quiet. I asked him what he was thinking about, and the following came pouring out of his heart: "Hey, Dad, let me tell you something. All my friends are telling me how it's okay and they're praying for me. That it's going to be all okay; it's just baseball, a game. But I'm telling you it's not okay. It's my dream. It's my brother and me! If God did this, I can't

176

stand him. If the devil did this, God is weak. And if God can't do anything about it, I don't ever want to be around God again. I'm done."

We pulled into the driveway and parked. He got out, slammed the door, and walked over to lock his car, a 2000 Buick Regal we called the "Beagle." It was a junker. The front seat was held up by a two-by-four jammed into the backseat. I had no idea why he even locked it. I guess maybe he needed some distance because he was saying the things to me that he was scared of saying or didn't dare say at church to his friends.

I walked into a semicircle of light at the edge of our garage, and he walked from the dark of the driveway to the edge of the light. Before I could say anything, he said, "Hey, Dad, I don't mean all that I'm saying so much, but I've got to say it, and I know you can handle it."

I put my hand on his head and said, "Look, I don't know the answers. I don't understand what's happening. I just know I'm in it with you and I'm not going anywhere." And we went into the house.

When our children hold the flag brave and true, we can experience an onrush of things we don't want to hear. Our children will protest what's happening in their lives. We need to understand that at its core protest is not a question of respect. It's about openly struggling with their hearts. If our children are able to find and use their voices, they will much more likely help other people, become advocates for other people to have their voices, and stand firm with other people. If they don't have their voices, they are not going to live by the ancient standards of love, nobility, and honor. Those ancient standards will become just an act that is about their outsides. They will know how to act right and behave but will not know how to live and love.

Realizing That Behavior Is Not the Goal

As our children hold the flag brave and true, they need to know that doing so is not about following a rigid code of expectations and behaviors. Behavior codes can be a good thing, but behavior codes are not the highest articulation of what we are to live out as human beings. We are called to love, not behave. We are called to courage and character. As children grow, parenting with a focus on behavior (not character) requires increasing levels of bribery, power, threats, punishment, and abandonment. Parents become police officers or taskmasters rather than guides.

The more rigid and controlling the code that governs behavior in our families, the more stunted our children will be emotionally and spiritually. Children can get really good at behaving well. Parents can force behavior with popsicles or by threatening abandonment with lots of shame and fear.

Our kids might say "Yes, sir" and "Yes, ma'am," but they won't have true respect. Remember Eddie Haskell from the 1950s television show *Leave It to Beaver*? Eddie has become a cultural reference of sycophantic behavior. Eddie was known for his well-groomed appearance and manners that hid a shallow, self-serving, and sneaky character. Typically, Eddie would greet Wally's parents, Ward and June Cleaver, with exaggerated proper manners and kiss-up compliments such as "That's a lovely dress you're wearing, Mrs. Cleaver." Eddie behaved well, but in truth, he was a weasel.

I (Stephen) was speaking at an elite private school several years ago. I remember that I was struck by the number of "Yes, sirs" and "No, sirs" and "Pleases" and "Thank yous" I encountered in the first few minutes. The administrator of that school proudly told me how well behaved the students were and how they had recently won a Bible trivia quiz bowl competition. A few weeks later, I learned that a majority of the students from the upper classes of that school were arrested at a party. The school leaders were rocked when they learned that drug and alcohol use and casual sex were the norm behind the scenes.

A board member of the school called for feedback and advice (one of his daughters and his son were involved). In our conversation, he seemed more upset that his kids had gotten caught than that there was a systemic character issue in their community or that he didn't really know his own children. To his credit, when we discussed that reality, he acknowledged with a sigh, "I guess I've been majoring on the minors." By that he meant he had been focused on the outside behaviors, not the heart. He, and the school he had chosen for his children, had taken the code of respect and turned it into a performance-based identity. When we lose the voices of our hearts, the only thing left to do is give our best performance or rebel.

At the same time, having no standards or having standards that are confusing and inconsistent similarly equals neglect, abandonment, and harm. This is more obvious than the neglect of "solid" expectations but just as harmful. Having no boundaries or adopting standards that say "Whatever I believe is okay as long as it doesn't hurt anybody else" leaves children adrift, and they are left to figure out their own lives.

They have nothing to push against and nothing to question. They feel alone.

A Parenting Paradigm

To best help our children "hold the flag brave and true," it is advantageous for us to better understand the internal motivations and stances we adopt as parents. One of the most difficult challenges of parenting with heart is creating a culture that is open enough for children to learn how to express their hearts but with enough boundaries to provide safety inside the values of loving self, others, and God. Our children need room to learn, grow, and then mature. They must also be rooted in values that are bigger than they are. When we as parents keep things simple and create boundaries and guidelines, our children have a container in which to grow. As parents, we fall within a paradigm based on two continuums. How these continuums intersect creates a paradigm for parental awareness and growth. Where we find ourselves in this paradigm can give us insight into how we need to continue to grow as parents. Please remember that parenting and growth are lifelong experiences.

The first continuum is between a parent-centered style and a child-centered style. That continuum intersects the second continuum, which is between a laissez-faire style and a hands-on style. Every parent is somewhere on these two continuums. Each side of the continuums has its own gifts, limitations, and dangers. In the paradigm created by the continuums, no quadrant is better than another, but the farther away we are from the center point, the less heart-focused we are as parents.

Parent- or Child-Centered Style

With a parent-centered style, the energy of the parent is about the parent. "I'm the boss." "I get to pick the radio station." "Because I said so." "This is the way it's going to be." A word that sums up this posture is *strength*. In this style, the parent is the authority in the child's life. The benefit of this approach is that the child can rest in the confidence and safety of the parent's strength. However, strength has its limits, and at times, parents who have a lot of this energy can be overbearing and/or unsympathetic.

On the other end of the continuum is the child-centered approach. Here the parental energy is largely directed toward the child. A word that summarizes this posture is *tenderness*. "Sure, dear. Whatever radio station you want to listen to is okay with me." "Of course I'm more than happy to drive you around and bring you things you left at home and help you even though I'm tired." "Oh, you coughed; come here and let me feel your forehead." The benefit of this style is that the child knows they are supported and cared for and have a soft place to fall. The downside to this posture of parenting is that the child can have too much power in the family. The farther the parent moves this direction on the continuum, the less the child will be able to develop resiliency and courage.

Laissez-Faire or Hands-On Style

A laissez-faire parent tends to be more relaxed and permissive. Thus, they avoid the trap of micromanaging the child. The freedom they offer the child can go a long way in helping the child develop their own ideas, confidence, and identity. The child typically has the room to express a broad range of emotions and learn from their own actions. With this style, the child is allowed to set their own boundaries, such as when they will go to bed, what they will eat, and whether or not they will do their homework. One risk is that too often mom and/or dad are more like a friend than a parent. Another is that without boundaries and limits, the child will often indulge themselves and will become entitled. The child who is used to having things their own way will have a much harder time when they encounter a system that is highly structured and in which rules are enforced. Research has shown that children of parents who never said the word *no* are more likely to get into trouble with the police and abuse drugs and alcohol when they are older. There is a serious danger when a child is given more freedom than they are ready to handle.

A hands-on parent tends to be more structured and engaged. They are involved in the details of the child's life. They are very responsive to what the child needs. In varying degrees, they also have expectations and agendas about what they believe is best for the child. A parent farther out on the continuum can become a tiger parent or a helicopter parent. The child often stays busy with full schedules of activities, lessons, and tutors. Their life is programmed. If the parent uses a lot of control, the child can struggle to function outside their routines or in new settings. The child can struggle with depression and anxiety and even have poor social skills. When the hands-on parent is too involved, they will overparent and become controlling. When this happens, the parent is energized mostly by their fear and attempts to save the child from having to experience life.

Combining these two continuums creates a paradigm that can give us some clarity on who we are as parents, how we need to grow, and what we might need to change. Where are you in this paradigm? Take a moment to graph yourself.

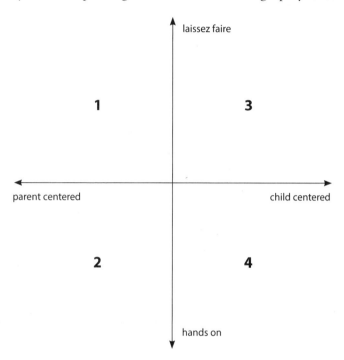

The Four Quadrants

Quadrant 1: Parent-Centered and Laissez-Faire Styles

The primary motivation of a quadrant 1 parent is the child's independence. The strength of the parent is that the child learns the world does not revolve around them. The child gets to see a grown-up who has their own dreams and passions. The child also is allowed to make mistakes, learn from them, and stand on their own two feet. The weakness of this quadrant is that the child can feel lonely and unimportant. Sometimes the child needs more than either the child or the parent can recognize. If you are a quadrant 1 parent, you are probably not reading this book; your spouse is reading this section to you. Another challenge is that the parent can end up being in competition with the child for the resources of the family.

Quadrant 2: Parent-Centered and Hands-on Styles

The main motivation of a quadrant 2 parent is the child's success (based on whatever the parent defines as success). The upside of this quadrant is that the child stays busy, accomplishes a lot, makes good grades, and has a great deal of success. The heart of the parent is fixed on wanting the child to have the most the child can. The parent wants the child to achieve so that the parent can be proud, reassured, and secure. The weakness is that the parent tries to control the outcomes. The child ends up being neurotic and anxious. They can be a very good pretender. Even if they are a great performer on the outside, inwardly they can be a mess emotionally and spiritually. Children who are a product of a quadrant 2 parent get stuff done, make great grades, and become leaders and doctors and lawyers, but they struggle to feel as if they are enough.

Quadrant 3: Child-Centered and Laissez-Faire Styles

The goal of a quadrant 3 parent is for the child to be happy. The child knows they are important, known, and understood. There is very little conflict in the parent-child relationship. But the parent has a hard time letting the child struggle and suffer. Feelings and needs are not allowed to go unsatisfied.

The farther out in the quadrant the parent is, the less parenting there is, and the child can mostly do whatever they want. Like Dudley in the Harry Potter series, the child is the master.

Quadrant 4: Child-Centered and Hands-on Styles

A quadrant 4 parent is motivated by their desire for the child to feel secure. In such a family, the child knows they are loved and are receiving guidance and input into their life. The child can have a fair amount of success and is very supported by the parent—even when the child doesn't succeed. Often, however, the child is not encouraged to take many risks. In addition, the parent can have a difficult time seeing and confronting the darker aspects of the child's personality. Ultimately, the child can end up taking on the emotional responsibility of the parent's well-being.

Where Are You?

It is rare in a two-parent family system for both parents to be in the same quadrant. We need to ask ourselves where we are and what we need to do to improve so that we can engage our children more full-heartedly.

Here is a personal example. I (Stephen) am in quadrant 1 (parent centered/laissez faire), while Heather is in quadrant 4 (child centered/hands on). The upside is that we can be a really good balance for our children. We approach our children from such different postures that we each offer them some really good things. I can give our children things she can't and vice versa. But the limitations are there too and cause conflict in our marriage.

At times, I can parent more out of shame, and Heather can parent more out of anxiety. I want to know if I'm going to be okay, and she wants to make sure our children are okay. My repentance as a parent is always toward what is going on in my children's lives and how I can show up more effectively and be fully present as a grown-up. Heather's repentance is always more toward herself and her dreams about her life—how she can practice self-care and become more comfortable with letting our children be discontent.

One of the paradoxes of parenting is that if we want to grow as parents, we have to address ourselves first and not our children. As parents, we have to be willing to see the log in our own eye. When we can identify where we are in the parenting paradigm, we can see where we need to grow in order to help our children keep the voices of their hearts. Hopefully, you can see yourself in this model and ways you can grow as a parent.

Helping our children hold the flag brave and true is about being in relationship. Children need our ongoing permission to be able to continue to articulate what is in their hearts. They need our help and guidance to be able to express what is happening within them. They need permission to say to us what they can't say anywhere else—especially if doing so leads us into our own struggles and questions.

Much of what we need to turn to and face as parents is what we don't want to see and don't want to name. Are we asking honest questions? Are we willing to turn toward ourselves and God in the process of becoming more of who we are created to be? When we do, we will be better able to help our children keep and grow the voices of their hearts. We will be free to stay with them in the process. We will continue to grow alongside them as they grow. We will recognize that the questions of their hearts are our questions too. We will be good-enough parents as our children walk the quest of living their own lives and possibly becoming good-enough parents themselves.

GOING DEEPER

- Write down ways in which you are each type of parent. Your style can even be somewhat different depending on the child. How does your style of parenting benefit your children? Harm your children? Hurt or help your marriage? Share your thoughts with your spouse and ask for feedback.

- Answer your children's questions. Take the time to respond, even if the response is "Please ask me that again tonight at dinner. I am late for work but want to talk about that with you." Be honest if you are rushed/distracted/overwhelmed. Kids typically know more than we give them credit for, and kids, like adults, recognize and usually appreciate the truth.

- Make a list of rules you and your spouse have for your children. Talk together about which ones come from a place of fear or worry that your children's behavior won't be what the neighbors/grandparents/Sunday school teachers expect it to be. Talk about which ones come from places where you felt unparented in your own childhood. Evaluate which ones to keep and which ones to begin letting go of.

NINE

Learn to Live the Questions

*If you could imagine the most incredible
story ever, it would be less incredible than
the story of being here. And the ironic thing
is that story is not a story, it is true.*

John O'Donohue

Parenting exposes our hearts to some of the most important questions in life because it involves relationship in which we risk the full depths of love. Some family friends of mine (Stephen's) volunteered to do mission work at an orphanage in Haiti. During the course of their time there, one of the children captured their hearts. Ferlando was a playful and charming three-year-old boy. While my friends and the boy spoke different languages, their affection toward him and their bond with him developed quickly. Over the next several months, they often traveled with their adolescent children back and forth to Haiti from the United States to work in the orphanage and to visit Ferlando. It wasn't long before they began to wonder as a family about adoption—first individually, then aloud with one another. There was one significant problem: Ferlando had a very aggressive and terminal illness.

In spite of the sickness, they eventually brought him to the United States for treatment and into their home to care for him as their own son. After many weeks in and out of the hospital, hours of consultation with doctors, and even more hours in prayer, Ferlando lost his battle with cancer. The process of loving this boy changed their lives dramatically and left their hearts full of questions. Why would *we* be called to this? Are we doing the right thing? What is God up to? Why would God lead us into something that was so painful? What good can come from a boy dying? What is normal now?

While the questions you may have as a parent may not be this poignant at the moment, the story you are called to live as a parent is wild and potent. If, as a parent, you are willing to live fully and love deeply, you will always have more questions than answers. How you learn to live the questions will have a great impact on your relationship with yourself, your children, and God.

Love Is Difficult

Our children, even in their smallness, vulnerability, and neediness, have the incredible power to impact our hearts. If our hearts are open to love freely, we will be captured by a love that is more powerful than we could have ever imagined. And we can't help but be changed. Because our children are a part of our very being, our love for them has a power over us that we will grapple with for the rest of our lives.

The love we as parents have for our children will unbalance and expose us emotionally and spiritually because it awakens us to how little control we have in our lives. One of the greatest spiritual gifts of being a parent is that it awakens us to our powerlessness and our need for God. Our hearts' desires and our capacity to make them come true are in great conflict. We want more than we can create. This exposes us to our powerlessness and neediness and unsettles us. It is supposed to. The way we go about living in this tension matters.

As parents, we have an inevitable propensity to want to control our children's lives in order to make our own struggles more emotionally and spiritually manageable. Sadly, many of us succeed in doing so and end up living in a hazy reality that is a dim version of how full our lives can be. However, when we are drawn to really pay attention to our lives, the haze can lift, and we can glimpse the amazing abundance of what we have been given to enjoy and to love. Sadly, it is often in sorrow and fear that we see most clearly the truth of our lives. God is faithful to pursue us to wake us up and invite us into the lives we are created to live. Most often the truth of life comes to us when we least expect it. And when this happens, we are unavoidably faced with how much our children matter to us and how out of control our lives can be, all at the same time.

No matter how well we prepare, life will surprise us with wake-up calls. The phone will ring while we are going about our daily lives. Our hearts will be gripped by the reality of life, and we will suddenly be transported from our dreams of the way we want our lives to be into the way life really is.

We will be awakened from our distractions and reminded of what truly matters and what we truly love. In an instant, our fantasy of control will evaporate, and we will come face-to-face with the depth of our love and our powerlessness over life. In moments like these, life slows down, all our misplaced priorities fall away, and we are left holding on to what is most dear.

During these times, we have questions about ourselves. Will I be okay? Do I have what it takes to be a good-enough parent? How do I live fully? How can I help my children do the same? Who am I becoming? How do I love them? How can I be loved well? Who knows me? How do I get more of myself? How do I struggle well?

And we have questions for God too. Where are you in all this, God? Will you be present with me? Do you accept me as I am and love me as I am? Can you handle me being angry and disappointed with you?

It is a profound paradox that while these moments of truth offer us emotional and spiritual clarity, they simultaneously bring more questions than they provide answers. None of us are immune from this life. As Samuel Beckett reminds us in *Endgame*, "You're on Earth. There's no cure for that."[1] Another way of framing Beckett's idea is that there are few if any answers to life's most important questions; even when we are fortunate enough to find answers, they don't satisfy us for long because new and old questions soon begin to surface. There is no answer to make love safe, and there is no way we can place life under our control. Although God is with us, Emmanuel, we are not at home in this place called the world.

My (Chip's) wife, Sonya, took our son William to an orthopedic doctor to get X-rays of his lower back. He was having pains that were preventing him from participating in sports. We also had some mild concern because he had congenital issues related to his back and hips. It was five o'clock, closing time, when the nurse came into the room looking concerned. Soon after, the doctor came in. He walked over to William and said, "Son, we have found a mass on your spine, some kind of tumor." Then he placed his forehead against William's forehead and said, "William, we are going to do everything we can to help you. We are not leaving you in this." He told Sonya that this type of tumor would require a specialization beyond his own comfort level. He said he would help us find the right person, whether that meant we would have to go to Baltimore or San Diego. By eight o'clock that night, he had found a specialist in Nashville, thirty miles from our home.

The fact that we were blessed to have a physician who could examine and then help William was such a relief. At the same time, our journey had just begun. We were full of questions. Will he be able to walk after surgery? Will he die? Does he have cancer? Are there more tumors? God, what does all this mean? Hasn't he suffered enough with other things? Are we cursed somehow?

When they took William from us into the operating room a month later, the low, quiet guttural sound coming from Sonya was the question cry of every parent. Will I see him again? How will he be without me? What do I do with the heart of my heart being pulled from me?

She and I were full of love's cost and powerless but for the prayers of many and the friends who surrounded us. I still remember how surprised and grateful I was that so many beautiful people cared so much for William and us.

The nurse told us the first question William asked when he came to was, "How is my mom?" I think he heard her love cry before they took him away. When we told him that the results of the surgery were even better than we hoped, slow tears rolled down the side of his face as he said sleepily, "Good. I was so scared."

William recovered from spinal surgery; he lives a full, vibrant life, thankfully. But even as I relive this story, tears come quickly because I know how much I love him and Sonya and Tennyson and how much I don't have control of life. I am still left with the questions that are in all of us who love and who know how little control we have. Why did everything turn out okay? What will happen next? How do I let myself care so much when I know that heartache is inevitable? God, when does the pain get better? What about all the people in worse situations? How will I grow to be able to face life on life's terms? God, how can you be bigger in my life?

Questions Lead Us

To borrow a phrase from John O'Donohue, our "questions hold the lantern"[2] to help us see our way through life. People who are wise of heart know that questions are more illuminating as guides through life than are answers. Good questions can carry us for years, while answers can often lead to dead ends. Any question we have about life is a good question, because it is going to lead to another question and another question and to some answers—that will inevitably lead to more questions. Our questions lead us to God, and we simply cannot live this life well without dependence on God.

We are not alone in our questions. Our children will ask similar questions throughout their lives. To help them in their questions, we need to be good at asking and carrying the tension of our own questions. As parents, the better we are at asking and living our questions, the more equipped we will be to help our children learn to ask questions and use them as guides in their lives. This is a far more contemplative approach to parenting than most of us are familiar with.

The questions about life that rise from our children's hearts will range from the general and philosophical (e.g., Why are people mean? Why do people die on Sundays? Why are some people poor and others rich?) to the personal and practical (e.g., Why did God let Grandma get sick? Why did Mommy leave? When will I die?). By not rushing to pat answers but staying connected to the hearts of our children through the beautiful and courageous questions that rise from their hearts, we will help them stay in touch with what they care about most and help them begin to see their individual character and passion and purpose.

Asking Better Questions

To ask better questions, we need two things: sensitivity of heart and honest curiosity. Because we are relationally driven beings, nothing moves us toward relational intimacy with ourselves, others, and God more than these two things. And nothing moves us away from intimacy faster than insensitivity and rigidity.

Sensitivity of heart does not mean being what some would call touchy-feely. It means being open to the internal emotional experiences of our own hearts and others' hearts, specifically our feelings, needs, desire, longings, and hope (see *The Voice of the Heart: A Call to Full Living*). To learn to ask better questions, we need to be increasingly willing to let the events of our daily lives affect us. Being sensitive of heart means we let life affect us or "get to us" because we are capable of truly caring. We are open to being moved, known, and inspired. But we are also open to being hurt, betrayed, abandoned, and disappointed.

When we have sensitivity of heart, we move from head-based questions to heart-based questions. Head-based questions most often begin with "Why?" These types of questions invite explanations and often justifications. Why does this hurt? Why do they act that way? Why do they do that? These why-type questions aren't necessarily bad, but they don't create much room for relationship. They aren't spacious questions. They aren't invitational. When we do get answers for them, the answers rarely satisfy our hearts because they always have "because" in them. "Because I said so" has never been a connector to the heart.

More heart-based questions such as "What?" "How?" and "When?" have the potential to open up new territories in relationship with ourselves, others, and God. These words work wonderfully in creating better dialogue with our children (and with anyone with whom we want better relationship, such as our spouses, family members, friends, coworkers). Imagine the difference in a conversation when asking a child "Why did you do that?" versus "What did you want when you did that?"

To ask better questions, we also need honest curiosity. The difference between honest and dishonest questions is that honest questions are questions to which we don't know the answers. Consider how many questions we ask our children that are really directives. "Are you going to pick up your shoes?" (Put your shoes away.) "How is your homework coming?" (I'm afraid you haven't been responsible with your time and not done your homework.) "Do you think I need to talk to your teacher?" (You seem to be having a hard time at school. That worries me. I am going to talk to your teacher to see if there is anything I need to do. It's important to me that you do well.)

Implied in all these questions are right answers and actions. Children aren't stupid. They know these veiled accusations aren't honest questions but rather techniques parents use to soften their requests, fears, or demands. When we wrap our statements in questions, we deliver messages in relational Rubik's Cubes, and our children ultimately have to guess what we mean. The vaguer the emotional content wrapped in the question, the more difficult it is for the parent and child to be close.

In contrast, there are no hidden statements in honest questions. Honest questions invite dialogue. They originate from a place of genuine curiosity. Honest questions don't assume an answer or an action. They give space for the person answering the question to articulate and expand and explore their own response. Asking honest questions will make our relationships more fulfilling and our lives more dynamic, though less predictable. Our lives will be more playful, wild, and joyful as well as more painful, confusing, and weighty.

Honest questions are open-ended. They can't be answered with yes or no. Here are some examples:

- What was that like for you?
- How did you wish for that to turn out?
- When have you felt that way before?
- Who are some people you know who are good at doing what we are talking about? Where have you seen them do it?

Some open-ended questions may scare off a child, especially a shy or introverted one. Other less heavy examples include:

- What do you like about being friends with _____?
- What is a job you think is interesting that you would never want to do?
- What is the best thing about being a child? What is the worst thing about being a child?
- If you had three wishes, what would they be?
- What are the best things and worst things about Mom and Dad?
- Would you rather not have media or chocolate for a year? Why?
- If you could travel back in time, when and where would you go?
- How would you describe your brother to your friends?
- What is the grossest thing you would eat?
- If you could change one law (or family rule), which one would you change and why?

Holding the Questions

Once we begin to ask better questions, then we need to become adept at holding the questions and letting them begin to carve out new room in our hearts. Holding the questions is challenging. When we stop trying to figure out our lives and the lives of those we love and start being present and feeling our lives and the lives of those we love, we become much more connected with what we feel and need and what they feel and need. While doing this does promote relational intimacy, it also invites more pain and conflict into our lives. But the hallmark of a great relationship is the ability to navigate conflict well. Holding the questions is the opposite of sweeping things under the rug and avoiding the truth and is akin to naming the elephant in the room, or stating the obvious that we wish to avoid.

There are four key elements of learning to hold the questions. These are imperative to experiencing the truth to which our heart questions are leading.

1. *Willingness.* This is the degree to which we are emotionally and spiritually receptive to being affected. It means taking the risk of allowing our hearts to be fully involved. The more willingness we have, the more open we are to being influenced and changed by the heart questions we carry.

2. *Patience.* This is the capacity to accept and tolerate the waiting. Most often the pace at which God moves seems really, really slow. The word *patient* comes from a Latin word that means "suffering." To be patient is to bear the burden of hope. The more heart centered a question is, the heavier it is to bear.

3. *Work*. This is the amount of emotional and spiritual energy we spend attending to our heart questions. It involves the tasks that are associated with the relationship at hand and the activities and thoughts required to deal with it well. Journaling, counseling, praying, receiving feedback, pondering, imagining—these are all ways we can do the work of holding the questions well.

4. *Time*. This is the indefinite, continual progress of life and our stories unfolding before us. So much of learning to hold the questions well involves giving them time to reveal the multifaceted truths toward which they are guiding us.

Here is an example of a heart question to hold and carry as a parent: How does my relationship with my mother influence how I relate to myself, my children, and God? A parent could spend a lifetime attending to this question.

Living the Questions

The questions our hearts are offering us are foundational building blocks of wisdom about life. Once we are asking better questions and holding the questions well, we can begin to live the questions one day at a time. Living the questions is about accepting, tolerating, and living in the mystery of life and letting this process guide the direction of our days. As emotional and spiritual creatures, we need an ever-growing appreciation for mystery. But because of our biology and our life experiences, most of us not only don't appreciate mystery but also stay away from it. Mystery is what we don't know and where we are made to go. Mystery is in the world of tomorrow. We detest ambiguity. We abhor ambivalence. We crave certainties. We look for guarantees. And we have reason to do so. However, that is not the essence of the lives we have to live. Our emotional and spiritual existence is a lot bigger than what we have ever imagined. We are created for eternity. We are made to inhabit a world of peace and joy without end, and yet we live in a world of endings and grief.

Scripture is full of paradoxes and doorways into mystery: "The kingdom of God is within." "The kingdom of God is like a child." "You have to lose your life in order to have a life." So much of the truth in Scripture draws us toward questions of the heart. Scripture is far more descriptive of the human experience than prescriptive of how to live it. There are no lists of what to give a spouse on their birthday. There are few details about what it means to honor a parent. Not much is said about how to handle conflict in a marriage. There is very little about what it means to parent a child through the totality of their life.

If we are not willing to ask questions and live in the mystery, we are going to end up living a very small, confined, controlled life. We are going to live a very immediate life—one of putting out fires. Everything is going to be about the next thing we can control and the next outcome we can produce. We will have a very short-term view of our lives and a very short-term view of our children's lives. Life won't be very spiritual. It will be ruled by to-do lists. It will be anxious.

Biologically Wired for Anxiety

Humans are biologically wired for fear. When you consider the following questions, what do you feel?

- What will happen next year?
- What will happen next week?
- What will happen tomorrow?
- What will happen to your children when they start to drive?
- What will happen to your children when they go off to college?
- What will happen in your parents' lives in the next ten years?

As you imagine the possible outcomes, you may notice that random negative and painful options pop into your mind. When most people consider these questions, they feel fear to some degree or another. They may call it feeling worried, anxious, apprehensive, or concerned, but these words are all different ways of expressing the emotion of fear.

When asked, "Of what are you afraid?" people will often answer, "The unknown." The problem with this answer is that, technically, we can't be afraid of the unknown. What we are really afraid of is bad things happening—again. Case in point: if there were a giant, hungry grizzly bear standing outside the door of your house and you didn't know it, you would not fear it—it's unknown.

When we consider the question "What will happen tomorrow?" we most frequently consider either the facts of our lives (the order of events) or negative outcomes. Rarely do we imagine something good happening—as if life were a game show. *When I wake up, I'll walk into my garage and balloons will be falling from the ceiling and people will be cheering and a new car will be parked in there.* That would be nice, but we don't make up such things. If we did, we would sound ludicrous.

We most frequently fill in the unknown with negative experiences because the human brain is wired to hold on to painful events more than it is wired to remember pleasurable ones. And the more painful the event, the more weight it carries in our decision-making and style of relating. All of human development has shaped the human brain to keep us alive. We have to have a mechanism that is on the lookout for danger. Part of our brain (the amygdala) functions like a prairie dog on alert, scanning the horizon for bad things that might happen. We are preprogrammed to be watchful for negative things. That part of our brain is assigned the critical task of asking two very basic questions: (1) What's going to happen next? (2) Will I be okay?

In response to those questions, another part of our brain (prefrontal cortex) is like a supercomputer and is really good at calculating all the possible outcomes. One challenge we have to deal with is that the supercomputer gives extra weight to the painful and negative events of our past experiences. So guess what we predict when we think about the future? Negative outcomes. When that happens, the prairie dog really starts working and scans the horizon even more. Then the supercomputer spits out even more negative outcomes. Before we know it, we have an anxiety loop that is feeding itself.

Left to just our biology, we become very anxious (and likely either controlling or avoidant as a result). But the more skilled we become at recognizing fear, addressing our past wounds, reaching out in relationship, and surrendering to God, the better we can transcend our biology and live fully out of our emotional and spiritual selves. We become more integrated and less anxious.

More Than Conquerors

There is something about becoming a parent that provokes questions. There is something about being a child that provokes questions. There is something about just living on this earth that provokes questions. Young children ask "Why?" all the time—and then their questions get more complex as they move through life. They move from questions about how things work to questions about their own origin, identity, and worth. Through these questions, they learn to struggle well.

Learning to live the questions well means that we, as parents, are able to show up emotionally and spiritually in the lives of our children, offer what answers we have, and be present to them in their lives. Outside of that process, our job, in so many ways, is to tell them about the struggles we had at their age and, as they mature, even about the struggles we have at our current age. In other words, we tell them about the full realities of what it means to live fully.

If we can be this kind of parent, our children will be more than conquerors. They will be able to face the trials of life with the certainty that they are not alone. They have the presence of their parents and a God who is faithful and true. They will approach the darkest moments with the confidence of knowing that we can be with them in the toughest questions (though it may break our hearts). They will know how to face life and will not try to defeat it because they know that nothing they can do can separate them from the presence of God's big love.

The way we can help our children through these moments of truth is by being people who are capable of asking, holding, and living questions well. Our ability to accept, willingness to enter into, and tolerance of life's mystery open doors for us to be with our children on deep emotional and spiritual levels. We can stay with them in the ups and downs of their entire lives. Our children cannot afford for us to pretend that they don't have heart questions. They need us to walk with them as they walk through their stories. They need to know that we are continuing to walk through our own. They need us to continue to expand our emotional and spiritual capacity so that we can help them move through their lives as they become full-hearted grown-ups.

GOING DEEPER

- What questions do you carry that you are resistant to address?
- Write down ten to twenty things that you love about each child. Then write down ten to twenty things that you struggle with about that same child. Pray about both lists.
- Make a list of the things you are grateful for in relation to your family. Include some that are about yourself, your spouse, your children, and your family as a whole. Be specific. These can be important things or things that seem small or insignificant. All of them matter.
- Be willing not to be in control. Have a child lead you on an afternoon adventure. They choose where to go (or if

you are in the car, which direction to drive). They decide the activity, the food, the music. Enjoy their pleasure of being "in charge." Spend some time later thinking about and then journaling about how it feels not to be in control, even when things are good. Imagine and then write about how it might feel when things are scary or hard. Share those thoughts with your spouse and see how their feelings are the same and how they are different. Ask your child, "What was it like being in charge? What did you like about it? What did you not like about it?"

TEN

The Ultra-Triathlon

Respect the distance or the distance won't
respect you! It will eat you up, spit you
out, and make you beg for mercy.

Unknown

An Ironman Triathlon is a long-distance race consisting of a 2.4-mile swim, a 112-mile bicycle ride, and a 26.2-mile run, raced in that order and without a break. It takes the average triathlete about 12 hours and 35 minutes to complete an Ironman. An ultra-triathlon is a triathlon of greater distance than that of an Ironman Triathlon. Thus, every ultra-triathlon must involve *more* than 2.4 miles of swimming, *more* than 112 miles of cycling, and *more* than 26.2 miles of running. The physical stamina needed for one of these races is equal to the emotional and spiritual stamina it takes to be a parent. Parenting with heart is like living in an ultra-triathlon. Because the challenge of parenting is so big, we need a long-term vision.

Parenting with heart requires a steady, present pace. Too often parents take a sprinter's approach and adopt a short-term view of life with their children. When we focus on the short-term outcomes of achievements and good behavior, we have a hard time helping our children develop the essential character they need to navigate life with passion, faith, acceptance, healing, intimacy, humility, forgiveness, and joy. When we parent with a focus on short-term outcomes, we are handicapping our children's futures. Even if they grow up to accomplish many good things that we are proud of as parents, they are in danger of missing the most crucial elements of what it means to be a person of heart. They will likely lack the integrity, wisdom, compassion, strength, courage, and temperance they need to be who they are made to be.

When my (Stephen's) second child, Elijah, was born, I was excited to have a son. I had grown a lot as a man since Emma Claire's birth two and a half years earlier, and I was eager to step into being the father of a son. Through the years, many people commented on how much Elijah resembled me. They called him my mini-me—which I loved, and he didn't seem to mind too much. As his personality developed, it became clear that our personalities were also very similar: strong, confident, assertive, a little bossy, engaging, good with people, thoughtful, and opinionated. He was my first son, and I saw so much of myself in him—all the things I enjoy about myself and many of the things I wish were different about me. At some point, I decided that I would do my best to keep him from developing what I deemed negative character traits. This was not so much a conscious thought, but it was something that was happening in our relationship. I wanted to be the best parent I could, and I wanted to make sure he got extra of what I perceived I didn't as a young man.

When Elijah was around six years old, he and one of his little brothers, Teddy, who was about three, were arguing over a stuffed animal puppy. They brought the argument to me to settle, each arguing their case as best they could. I felt this energy rise up in me that could best be described as my vow to "be the best parent." I quickly grabbed the animal and, playing the role of King Solomon, who threatened to cut a baby in half to learn who the rightful mother was, declared I would cut the animal in half if they didn't stop fighting over it, thinking that, as in the Bible story, the true owner would relent to let the puppy live rather than see it destroyed. What I didn't account for was that they were kids, not mothers. They continued to demand ownership of the puppy. So what did I do? I marched into the kitchen, opened the junk drawer, and pulled out a pair of scissors, giving them one last chance to come to their senses. I was going to teach them a lesson. When the arguing didn't stop, I took the scissors and cut the dog in half. They stared at me in shock and then both started crying . . . hard. It wasn't long before Heather got home and I, thinking I had done the right thing, proudly told her of my triumphant parenting moment, implicating my children for being at fault for the severed toy.

She looked at me with confusion, anger, and a look that said two things: "We need to talk" and "I should never leave you alone with the boys again." I didn't yet realize what a bully move I had made with my sons. I wanted to prove to myself I was a great parent, and in the attempt, I was left with a bruised ego and regret. I realized I was missing something but didn't know what it was. I had not yet come to see how committed I was to being right instead of being in relationship. Over time, with feedback from Heather and my friends, I began to loosen the grip on my pride and entered into letting parenting awaken me to how I need to change and grow. I continue to find out that what is in this book is true and real and doable. I've given up (most days) my need for my parenting to carry the weight of my identity, and I am accepting more and more that clumsy is as good as it gets.

A Crucible of HOPE

To be a good-enough parent, we must bring our hearts to the process of parenting. When we enter parenting full-heartedly, it becomes more about a process of our own maturity and sanctification than about the outcome of raising our children. In this way, parenting is an emotional and spiritual crucible of hope. A crucible is a pot in which metals or other substances are heated to a very high temperature or melted. The word has also come to mean a test, challenge, or difficult decision that forces people to change. Parenting is a crucible of its own kind. If we parent with heart, with a long-term vision, our hearts will be changed over and over again—and our true selves will be revealed in the process. The way we can stay in the process is to practice HOPE.

Honest. Truthfulness takes place through the language of the heart: feelings, needs, desire, longings, hope. The more we face and attend to the struggles of our own hearts, the abler we will be to live truthfully with ourselves and those in relationship with us.

Open. As parents, we need to remain open to feedback from those willing to give it. Feedback allows us to know more about ourselves from others' perspectives and helps us see what we can't see on our own. It gives us access to ways we can grow that we might be blind to otherwise.

Process. Parenting is not a fixed point but a dynamic growth evolution. Being a good-enough parent is not a result we obtain; it is more a rhythm we practice and an outgrowth we experience when we accept that life is unmanageable by ourselves, look to God, and surrender control. It is the way and the approach we take to live life on life's terms. It is how we allow life to happen for us. We attend to that by admitting powerlessness over life, surrendering to the God who made life, and accepting the care of God as life unfolds.

Experience. We need to do whatever we have to as parents to stop the insanity of autopilot parenting. Experience is knowing that life will leave an impression on us when we let it, or we can ignore it or defend against it. We are created to have great hope and be able to face loss. We are created to celebrate and grieve.

Parenting with HOPE helps us stay open to our hearts and the hearts of those we love most. We cease going through the motions of our lives and become available daily to our internal Spiritual Root System (feelings, needs, desire, longings, and hope). This allows us to be part of the bigger story we are made to live into with our children.

Parenting Changes You

Parenting is a heart-changing endeavor. To stay engaged over the long haul, we must let parenting become more of a spiritual practice than anything else. When our hearts are fully engaged, we discover that parenting is as much (or more) about our relationship with ourselves, others, and God as it is about our relationship with our children. When we as parents begin to see that parenting has as much (or more) to do with growing our hearts as people as it does with raising children, we discover that parenting is a continual unfolding process of confession, repentance, transformation, and celebration.

> *Confession.* Confession is the first step in becoming who we are made to be as people and parents. Confession is admitting to ourselves and others the exact nature of who we are (not so much what we have done). When this happens, we are exposed as human. It's important to understand that the word translated "confess" in the New Testament is most often a Greek term that means "to agree with." So confession really means to come into agreement with how God made us. Confession is the beginning of aligning ourselves with how God made us as emotional and spiritual creatures. When we live in confession, we can't help but turn back toward how we are made and turn toward the One who made us.

Repentance. Turning back to our true selves and to God is repentance. It has far less to do with turning away from something than it does with turning back toward something again. Parenting calls us over and over again to turn back to our true selves and to God so we can receive what we are made to receive—comfort, acceptance, courage, and peace.

Transformation. As we realign ourselves and turn back toward ourselves and God, we are changed. We find ourselves no longer in the trap of black-and-white thinking. We become patient. Our perspective on life has a longer view and is less myopic. Our vision becomes clearer, and our actions can follow.

Celebration. Celebration has two components: delight and gratitude. Delight is the expression of joy in being willing to let ourselves give and receive love. Gratitude is a gift we receive when we can trust that God is in control of the outcomes and accept that God is faithful.

This rhythm and process of confession, repentance, transformation, and celebration is a continual homecoming. We continue to return to the heart of the matter, the heart of who we are, and continue to keep finding the courage to live life on life's terms. When we show up emotionally and spiritually, one moment at a time, our lust for predictability and the status quo fades. We benefit from accepting that life is really about continuing to change and growing into being able to love better and better.

If we are people who are growing, then we will be parents who know to stay in conversation with our children because we know they can teach us a lot. And when there is conversation, parents and children have the ability to share their hearts with one another as daily life keeps happening. Wise-hearted parents are people who are willing to learn about life from their children because parenting is not about being perfect. It's not about being a parent. It's about being a person who can parent. We have to be people who are open to being changed so that our hearts can keep growing alongside those of our children.

In this way, being a good-enough parent is about giving ourselves permission to extend grace to our children and to our spouses—giving what we have received. In parenting with heart, we are not playing the short game. If we don't give ourselves a break for messing up, we will wear ourselves down. We need to allow ourselves to begin again each morning. Our children are resilient. They don't expect or, more importantly, actually need perfection. What they do need is a parent who shows up—warts and all—over and over and over.

Our children need parents who are really good at both sides of forgiveness. They need our "I'm sorrys" when we mess up, and they need our grace when they do. They need us not to condemn ourselves for our yesterdays so that they can enjoy being with us today. When we judge ourselves and have contempt for ourselves, we cannot have relationship with our children.

Children need examples of what it's like to live well despite the mistakes we as humans inevitably make. We are a highly fallible species. If we can somehow manage to get our egos out of the way, our human frailties point our children to God. Our finite energies, our limited perspectives, our hard hearts, and our hurtful tongues are, oddly enough, ways of showing our children that we alone are not enough for them—that we alone cannot heal their hurts, fill their emptiness, and change their hearts. Also, by giving up our unrealistic need to be "the perfect parent" for our children, we are really freeing ourselves to love them well—to simply delight in who they are and have gratitude that we are with them.

Parenting is a long series of good-byes. The heartbreaking proposition of being a parent with heart is this: "I'm going to give you everything in me so that you can take it and give it to someone else." When we parent with heart, we are equipping our children to leave well. If we are good-enough parents, then our children are going to be equipped to love others (i.e., their own spouses and children) in ways they never loved us. They are going to want to be with them more than they want to be with us. If they don't, then something is off and they will not be free to give their hearts to someone else.

Slowing Down

Seeing parenting as a long view slows us down. We begin to notice and delight in the small things. Life takes on more meaning, or more accurately, we become in tune with the deeper meanings of life. The fast approach to life makes us hurried and worried. There is a direct correlation between how busy our lives are and how superficial our relationships are. This is especially true in our relationships with our children.

When we are busy, overprogrammed, and hectic, we become focused on the circumstances of life instead of the substance of life. Busyness puts our emotional and spiritual lives in conflict with the activities of our lives. This busyness can become so extreme that we lose contact with who we really are and how we are really made.

To stay present with our true selves and our children, we need to daily admit our feelings and needs, surrender to the process of God in our lives, and accept the outcomes. The better we get at admission, surrender, and acceptance, the more freedom we will find to be able to offer our hearts to our children and to help them keep theirs. We end up living out Reinhold Niebuhr's famous "Serenity Prayer":

> God, give me grace to accept with serenity the things that cannot be changed, courage to change the things that should be changed, and the wisdom to distinguish the one from the other. Living one day at a time, enjoying one moment at a time, accepting hardship as a pathway to peace, taking, as Jesus did, this sinful world as it is, not as I would have it, trusting that You will make all things right, if I surrender to Your will, so that I may be reasonably happy in this life, and supremely happy with You forever in the next. Amen.

Notes

Chapter 1 Giraffes on Ice

1. D. W. Winnicott, *Playing and Reality* (UK: Tavistock Publications, 1971).

Chapter 2 Wired for Relationship

1. Chip Dodd, *The Voice of the Heart: A Call to Full Living* (Nashville: Sage Hill Resources, 2014).

2. Chip Dodd, *The Needs of the Heart* (Nashville: Sage Hill Resources, 2016).

3. John Bowlby, *Attachment and Loss*, vol. 1 (New York: Basic Books, 1969); M. D. S. Ainsworth, M. C. Blehar, E. Waters, and S. Wall, *Patterns of Attachment: A Psychological Study of the Strange Situation* (Hillsdale, NJ: Erlbaum, 1978).

4. J. M. Gottman and R. W. Levenson, "A Two-Factor Model for Predicting When a Couple Will Divorce," *Family Process* 41, no. 1 (Spring 2002): 83–96.

5. S. Carrere and J. M. Gottman, "Predicting Divorce among Newlyweds from the First Three Minutes of a Marital Conflict Discussion," *Family Process* 38, no. 3 (Fall 1999), 293–301.

6. J. M. Gottman, "A Theory of Marital Dissolution and Stability," *Journal of Family Psychology* 7, no. 1 (June 1993): 57–75.

Chapter 5 Failure Is Not Optional—It's Inevitable

1. These characteristics were discussed by Dan Allender while Stephen was attending graduate school at Mars Hill Graduate School, Western Seminary, Seattle, 2001–3.

Chapter 6 Put On Your Own Mask First

1. Jeffrey M. Jones, "In US, 40% Get Less Than Recommended Amount of Sleep," Gallup News Service, December 19, 2013, http://news.gallup.com/poll/166553/less-recommended-amount-sleep.aspx.

2. Herbert Benson, MD, and Miriam Z. Klipper, *The Relaxation Response* (New York: HarperCollins, 2009).

3. M. R. Salleh, "Life Event, Stress and Illness," *Malaysian Journal of Medical Sciences* 15, no. 4 (October 2008): 9–18.

Chapter 7 Climb the Mountain of Their Dreams

1. Stephen James and David Thomas, *Wild Things: The Art of Nurturing Boys* (Carol Stream, IL: Tyndale, 2009), 200.

Chapter 9 Learn to Live the Questions

1. Samuel Beckett, *Endgame* (New York: Grove Press, 1958), 53.

2. John O'Donohue, "The Question Holds the Lantern," *The Sun*, November 2009, https://www.thesunmagazine.org/issues/407/the-question-holds-the-lantern.

Stephen James is the founder and executive director of Sage Hill Counseling and has been a psychotherapist in private practice for nearly two decades. He has taught many seminars on marriage and parenting from the heart. The author of five previous books, including *Wild Things: The Art of Nurturing Boys*, Stephen has a master's degree in counseling from the Seattle School of Theology and Psychology and a bachelor's degree in English from Belmont University. He and his wife, Heather, have four children, Emma Claire, Elijah, and twins Henry and Teddy.

Chip Dodd is a counselor, teacher, and author who has been working in the fields of recovery and redemption since 1988. He holds a PhD in counseling from the University of North Texas and a master's degree in English from the University of Mississippi. In 1996, he founded the Center for Professional Excellence at Journey Pure in Murfreesboro, Tennessee, to help professional men recover from addictions, anxiety, and depression through a holistic, multidisciplinary approach to treatment. His influential book, *The Voice of the Heart: A Call to Full Living*, was published in 2001 and has helped people transform their lives and relationships through a return to the heart and its core feelings. Chip and his wife, Sonya, have two grown sons, Tennyson and William.

Connect with **Stephen James**

Stephen is the founder and executive director of Sage Hill Counseling.

You can find out more and read the blog at
SageHillCounseling.com

 @StephenBJames | Stephen James, LPC-MHSP, NCC

Connect with **Chip Dodd**

Visit Chip online at **ChipDodd.com**
for podcasts, videos, a blog, and more!

Chip is the founder of the Center for Professional Excellence
at Journey Pure in Murfreesboro, Tennessee.

You can find out more and read the blog at **SageHillResources.com**

 ChipDodd    ChipDoddPhD   ChipDodd